Praise for *Three-Letter Words*

"Niall and Glen simplify personal development so that it's accessible to everyone. You'll love their humour and ability to get you to take action whilst appreciating more about life."

-A.N.OTHER
Author of Another Book about Stuff

"If you're looking to improve your life and not sure how to do it, this book is the one you need to read."

-U.KNOWWHO
Leading thinker in whatever

"Together they've distilled the psychology of personal change into a usable guide that you can start implementing today. Buy it, read it, and start putting it into practice and your life will be better!"

-A.SUCCESS
Leadership Guru

"Buy it, you'll love it."

-B.YOURSELF
TV Presenter and Celebrity

Ok, so we've had a bit of fun here but if you or someone you know reads this book and would like to have your name included above then please get in touch.

Three-Letter Words That Can Change Your Life

First published in Great Britain in 2017

Copyright © Glen Butler & Niall Lavery 2017

The moral right of the author has been asserted.

ISBN: 9781520526584

About the authors

Niall & Glen have spent the majority of their professional lives working in the field of personal development as trainers, facilitators, coaches, designers and authors. They take their work seriously but you'll rarely find them being too serious as 'life's too short' is definitely one of their mottos.

Their first book 'Brilliant Basics for New Trainers' took their combined 30 years of training and gave people all the advice and help they wished they had had earlier on in their careers. This new book has a much wider scope as they want to encourage even more people, people like yourself to take charge of their own personal development, not just by reading books or attending training courses but by changing small parts of their day to day lives so that they live a more varied, interesting, exciting and fulfilling life. You will not find much theory or scientific evidence in this book as they believe that 'if it works, it works!' Give it a go and if it works for you then great! If it doesn't, try something else! How many people do you know that do not have a clue how the engine in their car works but are happy to turn the key and get going? This book is your key, you're the engine, you have all you need.

So on that note, let's get going...

Contents

Introduction

Getting you started, it's as simple as ABC.

Chapters

'You have brains in your head.
You have feet in your shoes.
You can steer yourself in any direction you choose.
You're on your own, and you know what you know.
And you are the guy who'll decide where to go'

Dr. Seuss

Introduction

Hey! What a simple 3-letter word, but think of its power. That 3-letter word might be the very first word you say to your future husband or wife, or your new best friend. Every day the words we choose to use or say can and do have a massive impact on the rest of our lives. 'Hey!' might be the word you say to let an existing loved one know that you are there for them when life throws one of its 'oh-so-regular' challenges at them.

So, "Hey" to you, our reader. You have said yes to picking up this book, probably judging it by its cover or maybe its title. Well how else do we choose what to read? Hopefully a good friend recommended it to you and if they did, please do the same if you like it. However, you have come to be here, we truly believe you have made a great decision. You want change, change for the better. That doesn't necessarily mean tomorrow you will be quitting your job, selling your house and travelling the world in search of 'inner peace'. Do let us know if you find it as we would love to know where it's been hiding all these years. What it does mean though is that you know that positive change is something that each and every one of us is not only capable of but something that is essential in the modern world.

Change happens all the time and if you don't change with the times you will soon get left behind, stuck in a rut, doing the same thing you have always done, getting the same results. Our aim in this book is to help you change your life for the better using proven, questioning and actions. Helping you map out not just where you want to go but also how to get there.

Why 3-letter words?

This book is about keeping things simple, 3-letter words simple. Although short, many of them can be and are very powerful. We have looked at words that really can change your life. What is it like to be in 'awe' of something? How short a life would we have without 'air'? Or consider for a moment, what life do you want to live before you 'die'? Short, yet powerful. And simple is far easier to remember than complicated. Once you remember the words then you can focus on making each one work for you. If you can't remember something how on earth can you ever be expected to use it?

How many? According to where you look and whether you're a fan of the Oxford English Dictionary or a Scrabble player there are approximately 1000 3-letter English words. Ok, so we're not about to ask you to understand each and every one of them (read the dictionary if that's what you really, really want to do) but we would like you to focus on just a few, fifty-two in fact.

Why 52?

This book is about getting you to act (more on this fab word later), to take actions designed to change your life for the better. We think one of the most effective ways of doing this is to take action each and every week. Next week will come and go whether you like it or not, and the one after that, and the one after that. Every week of every year you have the opportunity to make changes for the better, even if they appear to be tiny things over a period of time they add up to something special. It's up to you now whether you continue your existing patterns of behaviour, those habits you have got into or make changes. The exact journey is up to you: Either work through them in the order of the book or pick out what interests you most from the contents page, read the chapter and get yourself geared up to try something new! In this paragraph alone you have just read 43 3-letter words!

Why now?

Between us we have nearly 30 years of experience training, coaching, facilitating, mentoring and working with people, people like YOU. We have had the opportunity to work with some wonderful people who have opened our eyes and challenged our thinking, which in turn has meant we have changed our thinking patterns and habits and we are truly grateful to them for doing that.

We are also students ourselves, constantly researching and learning from new developments and thinking whether in neuroscience or psychology, business or leadership and vitally from our own life experiences. This does not mean we have got it right or perfect or are living enchanted lives but we know what works when we see it. We trust our experience as well as our intuition and love to share that with others. Yes, we have made mistakes. With hindsight we now realise the error of our ways. We have said and done things that we regretted later. We have failed to take advantage of opportunities and on occasion's squandered money and time.

The lesson is; never try to be perfect, after all, who is to say what perfect is? But do live your life with purpose, learn from the challenges as well as the successes and keep growing as a person.

Getting you started

How is your life right now? Perfect? Nearly perfect? A long way off? You may be reading this feeling frustrated as you know there's more to life, to your life. If you want things to change, YOU have to change. If your attitude is "I don't mind change as long as I don't have to change" then you'd better ask for a refund on this book quickly. Nothing will change unless you do. Strangely people don't always realise that personal development means 'change'. This can be starting new things, stopping others or maybe taking a different perspective. Maybe areas of your life don't need to change but your view of them does. That alone can be enough of a difference. To paraphrase William Shakespeare 'Nothing is good or bad but thinking makes it so'.

As you now get going we want to help you understand our three steps to personal change. Of course we've managed to explain it with 3-letter words (you had better get used to them!) because it should be as simple as ABC. Our approach is based on research we have undertaken in the area of personal development as well as our own experiences. It goes something like this...

A. You

Even though we will be sharing our thoughts, ideas and experiences with you, this book is all about you. As the airline video reminds you, 'always put your oxygen mask on before helping others'. If you make yourself the best possible version of you, imagine the impact that will have on others around you, your family, friends and colleagues. Our intention is to help you focus and develop both your thoughts and your actions. It's time to be selfish. Let others live their own lives for a moment and concentrate on you. This is not only an important component, it's the MOST important component. The choices you make today will shape not just tomorrow but every day of the rest of your life. It's up to you to make the choice. So, happy to do some work on you?

How did you just answer that question? Did you say "yeah, ok then I'll give it a go" or "I suppose that's true." Sorry, that's not enough. You're not taking yourself seriously enough. Anyone can read through this book, happily skipping from page to page getting to the end and then saying "right, what's next." Just reading the words means nothing. We want you now to say in a tone of excitement, passion and determination "I am so important that I will do whatever it takes to improve my life and I will read through this book looking for ideas." Your smile today can set off a chain reaction of positivity that you will never know about.

B. Hmm!

Have you ever considered what really goes on in your head? You know there's a brain in there but are you in control of it or does it ever seem to 'have a mind of its own' excuse the pun. What we aim to do here is help you take control of your brain, your thoughts, your mindset, your outlook and your life going forward by challenging your thinking. After some chapters we'll ask you to stop reading and do some thinking. As busy people we don't often spend time really thinking about what we want, how we live our lives or what we might change. That changes now. Stop, think and move on.

Of course our brains and bodies are completely connected and making changes to either one can and will affect the other. The famous sportswear manufacturer ASICS is an abbreviation of a Latin phrase "Anima Sana in Corpore Sano", which when translated into English means "a sound mind in a sound body", something which we believe is a great aim to have. Work on both.

So where are we going wrong? We're sure you've heard of or met people who are unhappy because they are overweight, so they eat for comfort, put on more weight and become even more miserable. The spiral continues or something stops it. Why do we often follow these negative spirals? Do we ever stop to listen to the voices in our heads, the stories we tell ourselves and challenge them? (Do you really have a 'sweet tooth' or is that just the story you tell yourself?)

Even though these stories and patterns of behaviour often make us unhappy we continue to do the same thing over and over again. The truth is they are often not as bad as we make them out to be in our own heads. They are often not 'reality'.

How about setting up new stories, positive ones? Maybe it's time to tell yourself that you are capable of change, you do have the skills, the motivation and support you need. This is not just 'positive thinking' but taking a more realistic view of yourself. Bringing yourself back into balance.

Being happier, more positive and content feels so much better. Our aim is to encourage you to think differently about yourself, the world and other people. Different thinking will bring you different results. Hmm….!

So one route is to change our thinking first. But can we also change but acting differently?

C. Act

So we can help with all that brain stuff and help get your head pointing in a better, more productive, more fulfilling direction, but is what is thought without action? The old phrase says "it's the thought that counts" but is it really? You can spend all day thinking what it is like to be a millionaire but you won't get rich this way. You can think about going on a diet and not lose a single pound or kilo. What you need to do is act. Take action! Go for it. Give it a try. Get started. Do something, anything as long as it's different to what you've done before. This book contains many suggestions of things you can do in your everyday life.

Often we wait around for our thoughts to change before acting. Yes, at times this works but did you think yourself into believing you could ride a bike? No. Like the rest of us you got on it and gave it probably several attempts, maybe fell off a few times and hopefully had some parental support and guidance. But once you'd done it, cycled along by yourself without any help, you truly believed it was possible. The action changed your mind about what was or wasn't possible. So some of the chapters suggest action. Don't put any thought into it, just do it.

Try something different, something new, especially something challenging and see how it affects you. Granted not everything will be positive, eating snails in a restaurant may leave you swearing to never do it again but your mind will have been changed.

You'll know that you're the kind of person that is willing to get out of their comfort zone and make a difference.

Your change plan

In summary, we will ask you to put you at the top of your priority list. Every week we'll ask you to stop, to go hmm to get you thinking about your life in a more positive way, to get you thinking differently. We'll also be getting you to act, to do things differently or maybe to do things you've never done before. Each suggestion we have for you is simply set up with a 3-letter word. Some may require planning and time, others are things you can start doing tomorrow, maybe today even. So act now rather than letting another opportunity slip through your fingers.

Three-letter Words

1. Yes

Say it out loud now "yes" and again "yes", now say it 5 times in a row "yes, yes, yes, yes, yes." How do you feel? A little more positive than 10 seconds ago? We thought so (well we know so from our research). 'Yes' is such as positive word so let us begin by using it more often. Say it with confidence, meaning, commitment and a determined smile on your face. The famous quote says "it's the things you don't do in life that you regret" so it is time to stop saying 'no' and start saying 'yes.'

What can you start saying "yes" to? Firstly, the importance of your own personal development. You have said "yes" to reading this book (well up to here so far anyway) which tells us you have some level of commitment but as we said earlier in the book, reading it is not enough. To gain real benefit you will need to say "yes" to taking action, trying out all sorts of new activities and behaviours to create the 'new you'.

'Yes' can seem like a scary answer to a question such as "will you marry me?" Or "should I do a parachute jump?" But it will be worth it in the long run. We have met many people who have been petrified of jumping out of planes but have done so and as soon as they get their feet back on the ground the first thing they say is "wow that was amazing, I want to do it again!". Every decision you make is the right decision for you based on what you know and how you feel at the time.

Ok, with hindsight you may think you could have made better decisions in your life but you couldn't... because you had not yet lived that experience to learn from it. From today say "yes" to new experiences and you will learn so much more. And you can quote us here "Those who learn, earn". Take the example of Richard Branson, he has been quoted as saying "If somebody offers you an amazing opportunity but you are not sure you can do it, say yes – then learn how to do it later!"

Just before we move on, you may be thinking 'is this not just positive thinking?'. No, absolutely not. We know that positive thinking alone doesn't work. Well not without a plan anyway. We know that fear, worry, concern and doubt all have a place in your thinking which can turn you towards "no" or "maybe" so the following chapters are in place to help you commit with a resounding and positive "YES!"

Hmm moment:

Stop! Think what you have said 'yes' or 'no' to in the past. Draw a line down the centre of a sheet of A4 paper, write 'yes' at the top of the first column and 'no' at the top of the other. Now start listing all the things you have said yes and no to in the past, take your time and really think about it. Are there any themes you can identify? Do you say yes to easy tasks and no to stretching ones? Do you say no to adventure and yes to comfort?

Are you now ready to move on to chapter 2? Yes, great!

2. Aim

What is your aim in life? Not sure? Ok let us keep it simple, what is your aim for tomorrow? For the next week? Still not sure? Oh dear, we've got news for you. Research shows that people in life who do not set goals generally earn less than those who do, feel less fulfilled in life and as Brendon Burchard calls it in his fantastic book 'The Charge', live a 'Comfortable Life'. Is that enough for you to just be comfortable? Surely you want more? You want to experience the joys of life, the highs, and the amazing experiences life has to offer. Well these don't come knocking at your door. You have to go out and seek them. When you know what you're striving for you are much more lightly to achieve it. Yes, be happy with what you already have but don't get stale.

Imagine for a moment that you have a bow and arrows and three archery targets set out in front of you, one close, one a long way in the distance and one somewhere in between the two. Your task is to hit as many as possible. Which do you aim at first? If you aim far away you're likely to miss, get disappointed and start telling yourself "I'm no good at archery" and then either fulfil your own prophecy by missing the others (we do love to prove ourselves right) or maybe not even try aiming for the others at all.

Burchard, Brendon. *The Charge*. Simon & Schuster, 2012.

If, however you decide to aim for the closest one first you're a lot more likely to hit it which will build your belief in your ability and encourage you to keep trying. As you try more your skill improves and hey presto! You're the next Robin Hood hitting targets further and further away.

Personal goals work in exactly the same way. Aiming only for far away goals will often leave you feeling disappointed and giving up long before you're anywhere near achieving them. What we're not saying here is not to have long term goals. They are essential to give you a real sense of deeper level of achievement and some things in life do just take longer. The key message here is to set short, medium and long term goals and aim to complete them in that order.

Short term goals. These can be for today/tomorrow, this week, month or the next 10 weeks but ideally not over 3 months, that's getting into 'medium' territory. Have a mix of timescales. Let's get you started simply… when are you aiming to complete reading this book? It's definitely a short term goal but what timescale will be achievable but also stretching for you? Make it too easy and it won't motivate you. Make it too stretching and you'll struggle.

Medium term goals. Usually from 3 months to one year these will be stepping stones to your long term goals so if it helps go there first and set them. If you're happy to get on with these then consider what you want to be different in the next year. Do you want to make changes to your relationships, your career or your health for example? Taking some key steps towards these aims really can start making a difference to your life in a fairly short period of time.

Long term goals. The biggies. Stuff that really gives you a sense of fulfilling real purpose, impacting not just your life but the lives of others around you. Yes, you may hate that interview question 'where do you see yourself in 5 years' time?' but that's probably because you haven't given it enough genuine consideration. Ok, you may not know what job you want to be doing then but you do need to have an idea of what kind of person you want to be. Setting out the 'future you' will help set you on the right track, the right one for the best possible version of yourself.

Deciding where to aim, whether the target or the distance (timescale) is a skill in itself that you'll improve the more often you do it, so start now and set yourself some goals. After all, you can't hit what you don't aim for. As Wayne Gretzky says: 'You miss 100% of the shots you don't take.'

Act moment:

Take 3 sheets of paper and title them Short, Medium and Long Term Goals. Consider both your work and your personal life and just start writing down some things you would like to achieve. It could be learning how to swim, learning a new language, travelling to a certain country, recording your own soundtrack, building a new home, getting a promotion, going to pottery classes or losing 5 kilos. Anything! We're not holding you to these so don't be concerned if you have too many or some currently seem unachievable it's just to get you focussing on what you really want, the first essential step in achieving it.

3. Now

You now know what you're aiming for. Fantastic. When should you take action towards these goals? Someday? "Someday I will get round to writing that book". Let's just check for a second; Monday, Tuesday, Wednesday, Thursday, Friday, Saturday, Sunday. No, there was definitely no 'someday' there. Now is a much better time to start or to keep going. After all, you can't live in the past or the future, you can only live in the present. The now.

It's great to be aware of the 'now,' where are you sitting now whilst reading this book? Are you comfortable? How deep or shallow is your breathing? How are you feeling physically and emotionally? Being in touch with how you are feeling now allows you to make changes to improve things. If you aren't aware, how can you possibly know to it's time to change?

So why do we put things off? And what do we put off? Sometimes it's the things in life we'd like to achieve, the new challenges, a change of career, learning a new language or skill, trying a new sport. Other things we put off are the dull, mundane tasks such as filling in a spreadsheet, doing the ironing, tidying up that spare room or clearing out the garage.

There can be many reasons why we put these things off; there's something more fun to do, something more easily rewarding (immediate pleasure from watching your favourite tv programme), they seem too big or we simply forget it as it's just an idea or thought in our heads.

Here's a simple guide to helping you get more out of the 'now', get things done, planned and make the changes to your life that you really want. We'd like you every day from now on to create 'now moments'. So what's a 'now moment'? Every day, several times throughout the day we want you to stop and say "NOW!" and consider three things:

1. Is what I am doing now helping towards my goals, dreams and desires? If not, what can I do differently?
2. What tasks or activities can I add to my to-do list now that would in the future help me learn, develop and increase my own personal growth?
3. How am I feeling right now? Am I feeling energised (physically and mentally) enough to achieve my goals? What could I do now to get myself nearer to that 10/10 score?

It's ok if you don't know the answers to all these questions right now, we'll be covering lots more about them throughout the book. The best thing to do now is just to start asking yourself the questions.

So, what we really want is for you to focus on the now while planning for the future. Be present. So often in today's society we let our imagination run amok with the 'What if...' question and more often than not, it's not in a positive frame of mind. Have you ever thought, 'What if it doesn't go well?' What if they don't like me?' 'What if...?' What if...?' Turn down the volume if the voice that asks these questions pops into your head. Actually do that, imagine the voice becomes quieter and quieter until you can barely hear it. Instead live in the moment, immerse yourself in what it is you're doing and enjoy the present, the now!

Also, there is no point dwelling in the past, it's done, gone, spent.... From each and every experience you encounter, learn from it and keeping moving forward. Now is the time you are reading this book, now is the time to do something, stop putting things off and telling yourself you'll do it tomorrow, because in some instances tomorrow is a very long time away. There is a Latin phrase 'Carpe Diem' which translates to 'Seize the Day.' What you decide to do now, will help determine where you want to be in the future.

Act moment:

In a moment we're going to ask you to stop reading and do something 'now'. Take a few seconds, a minute if you will and consider something you've been meaning to do for a while. It could be making a call to someone you know, fixing something, cleaning your bathroom, selling that old junk in your loft or reading that book on your bookshelf, you know, the one you bought but never finished. You may not complete the task but at least take some action towards it, after all the first step is usually the hardest. Go do it, NOW!

4. How

Great. So you have got an aim, something you really, really want to achieve and you know that now is the time to start taking action but there's something else stopping you, something niggling away, fear, doubt, insecurity or maybe you just don't know how to do what needs to be done.

Let's help with the biggest challenge first, your mindset. And when you've overcome this challenge, working out how to do the actual tasks is easy!

Often people who are not as successful as they would like to be see others having what they desire, more money, a bigger home, a better job, taking more holidays and generally getting more out of life and their inner voice says something like "well they had a better upbringing, lived in a nicer neighbourhood, went to a better college, have better connections or they're just luckier than I am". Sometimes it's not just their inner voice, you'll hear people say things like this in conversation. Do you think that this mindset helps you achieve your aims, dreams, goals and desires? Of course not.

This is why we need the 'how'. When you see others having what you want, stop and ask yourself "how can I....?" How can I have more holidays? Or how can I drive that sports car? Do make sure though that it is what <u>you</u> want and you're not just jealous.

Why should you ask 'how'? Because asking 'how' sets your mind along a very different path to the one that the 'complainer' has. Asking 'how' opens your mind to possibility, to challenge, and to options. Ok, so you won't immediately have the answer to your question but you're setting your brain up for longer term success, not a quick win. If it was that easy we'd all be driving Ferraris and living in mansions.

So you've got a helpful mindset, but what about the actions you need to take? After all, as Tony Robbins says 'walking into your garden shouting "no weeds, no weeds" won't get rid of them'. You'll need to start pulling and get your hands dirty.

One of the best ways to work out how to do something is to seek out others who have walked the path before you. They've trodden it down and carved out a route that for you is now much easier to follow. If your question is "how can I get rich?" then seek out rich people. Watch them. Read about them. Study them. Learn how they became rich. Was it through buying and selling goods or property? Was it through inventing something? Was it through providing services that others needed? Do this and you'll get a much better idea of 'how' you can get rich rather than staring at your latest bank statement and shouting "more money, more money!".

Robbins, Tony. www.tonyrobbins.com

If you're aim is to lose weight, get fit and be healthy then start hanging around with people who already fit that criteria. Find out what they eat and when, what exercise they take, how much water compared to alcohol they drink and how much sleep they get. Now you can start to build your own 'how' by simply copying them or selecting the bits that fit best for you. You really don't have to reinvent the wheel. Chapter 17 can help you too, it's called 'gym'.

'Each player must accept the cards life deals him or her: but once they are in hand, he or she alone must decide HOW to play the cards in order to win the game' Voltaire.

Hmm moment:

Look at one of the aims you wrote down in Chapter 2. Find a comfy chair where you won't be disturbed and sit and relax. Ask yourself, 'how can I achieve that aim?' Allow yourself a good 10-15 minutes just to let ideas swirl around your head ensuring you keep focused and if necessary repeat the questions, challenging yourself to come up with even more answers. One is definitely not enough!

5. Can

Have you ever bought an item in a store, then changed your mind and decided to return it, only to find that you lost the receipt? Yes of course you have, we think we all have at one time or another but hold on! 'It'll be alright as it's an own brand label they are sure to take it back' only to find that one cashier, you know the one we mean. The one who tells you, 'I can't give you a refund without the receipt!' Or 'I can't do that because it's not our store policy!' How infuriating is this? Often in life we focus on and tell people what we can't do. Let's change our focus from now on to 'What you can do?' Think for a moment how you would feel if today you made a list of everything you can't do. Then you added to that list every day. Imagine your state of mind after a few days, let alone a few weeks! Now imagine the opposite.

By focusing on the positive the, what can I do? Makes you feel so much better, so why not do it? As the quote attributed to Henry T Ford says "whether you think you can or whether you think you can't, you're right". Of course this doesn't mean you could say "I can run a marathon next week" and suddenly be fit enough to do it when you've put in no training. What we are saying is positive thoughts without action are no more than dreams. But positive thoughts will allow a degree of possibility.

Trying new skills, taking on new challenges will increase your 'can list' and not surprisingly make you feel better, resulting in more positive thinking in the future. It's more positive affirmation when we tell ourselves we can do something. How often have you told yourself or heard others say 'I can't do that!' or a shop assistant or customer service representative on the other end of the phone say 'Sorry I can't help you!' Michael Heppell in his fantastic book 'Flip It!' talks about reframing; it's a very simple concept when you think about it, we are much more positive when we tell ourselves 'I can do this!' 'I can master this!'

Life will present lots of challenges; in many different forms. The important thing to remember is to embrace these challenges, with a more positive mindset. As many call it, a 'can do' attitude.

Act moment:

Write down 3 things that you've considered doing but previously said "I can't do that". Write them out as "I can…. (whatever you chose)". This may be something like "I can hang wallpaper", "I can learn to cook interesting, healthy new meals" or "I can go on that dating website". These don't have to be massive life goals like hiking Everest or becoming a black belt in karate. Small steps achieved lead you to more confidence and the future ability to take on bigger challenges.

Heppell, Michael. *Flip it*, Skyhorse Publishing, 2013.

6. You

At the beginning of this book we told you to be selfish, to focus on YOU! Now we are going to take that to the next level. Here in our mind are two great quotes that we really love – Dr. Seuss: "Today you are You, that is truer than true. There is no one alive who is Youer than You." And the other by the Irish playwright, novelist and poet Oscar Wilde: "Be yourself, everybody else is taken". Bringing out that real 'you' rather than trying to be a version of other people around you or fitting the 'norm' whatever that is; will take a lot of wasted energy and time. So how do you make your own choices in life and truly be yourself?

We are not being totally selfish here though as you are not the only person in your life. The quality of relationships you have with others will make a huge difference to your life and you can choose how you will interact and engage with others. As Maya Angelou, the American poet and civil rights activist said "I've learned that people will forget what you said, people will forget what you did, but people will never forget how you made them feel." So how do you make other people around you feel? How do you choose to be with others? Is the 'you' that is reading this right now caring, considerate, and a person others choose to have in their lives because of the joy, love and all manner of other positive emotions that you have or are you someone who regularly argues, complains, belittles, and has a general negative impact on others?

Dr Seuss, *Happy Birthday to You!*, HarperCollinsChildrensBooks,1959.

'You' is a choice. Yes, the past has made us what we are now but the future, well the future; that is up to you. Life is a series of choice you can make. Make the right ones.

How 'you' are you? Do you do any/all of these the same as your parents: Read the same newspaper, vote for the same political party, follow the same religion, live in the same town, drive the same brand of car and eat the same food? Have you ever asked yourself "Am I my own creation?" then "If I were to design the perfect version of 'me' then what would I design?" How much confidence, ability or compassion would I include?

Act moment:

Take as much time as you need to write down (or draw a picture if you prefer) what the absolutely best possible version of you would look like. Done? Now consider how close your current reality is to this ideal version. If close, great. With just a few tweaks here and there that you have identified you will soon be living to your full potential. Keep reading to find a ideas to help you along the way. If your ideal self seems quite a way off from where you are now then think about this… the greatest journeys in life are not the short and simple ones. Your great journey starts here, now and you will have a bunch of amazing stories to tell once you have completed it. Of course, we hope you never actually 'get there' as a great life is about constantly learning and developing. Nobody we have ever met is perfect.

7. Try

Whatever you are doing now, STOP! (Pull over if you are driving and listening to the audio version, best not slam your brakes on!) Look around you and select any inanimate object. It may be a cup, a pen or your mobile phone. Pick it up. Now put it back down. Easy yes? Now look at it but don't pick it up. Easy again yes? Now look at it and 'try' to pick it up. Impossible right? You're either picking it up or you're not. There is no try.

Do not just take our word for it, if you are a fan of Star Wars movies and we are talking the original films you will probably have heard Yoda's wise words to Luke Skywalker, in 'The Empire Strikes Back': 'Do or do not, there is no try!' Ok, its movie land but his character and beliefs can be traced back to ancient wisdom from across the globe.

Try is weak, it is non-committal. It is your perfect excuse when you did not put in enough effort, commitment, energy, passion or planning. Imagine if Muhammad Ali had said to his opponents 'I will try to beat you" or Arnold Schwarzenegger has said "I will try to be the world bodybuilding champion". Instead both used the word will. The next time you are tempted with a 'try' response, either change it to a "yes, I will" or if your try was just avoiding something or trying to put it off, be honest and say "no, sorry I don't want to go to that corporate event" or "no, I definitely won't have time to get that done today".

Either way, yes or no, you're now committed to something, you are not just trying.

So when is it ok to try? Now we have said that try doesn't exist in the present moment, you could think about it in terms of reviewing the past. We can learn more effectively when we take time to review the past, what we have tried and enjoyed and/or found that we are good at or what we've tried and it just wasn't for us. Once though is not necessarily enough to try and give up. As a child you may have tried certain foods that you really didn't like only to try them later in life and find that you now like them.

You may have had a go at riding a bike and fallen off so you got on it again and again until you got to the stage where you can now ride. Imagine you have been on holiday to Italy and not had a particularly good experience. Are you going to say "well, I tried Italy and I didn't like it" or are you prepared to try again, maybe a different city, maybe a beach holiday, maybe skiing in the mountains? Don't let one unsuccessful 'try' put you off for good.

We say have a go, try something new. New experiences are fantastic, new foods, new drinks. Do you dip your toe or jump right in? Get out of your comfort zone, now for some this is easier than others, the thing is what level of risk are you comfortable with?

In a piece of research carried out and published in CAM (Cambridge Alumni Magazine) they studied individuals who had recently suffered a stroke. They carried out MRI scans to determine their brain activity and how big the affected area was. The researchers then divided the group in half, for half the study group they suggested that they go home, do nothing strenuous and recuperate from the event. The other half were told to read, exercise when possible, learn a new skill, they we asked to do crosswords and number puzzles. After a period of time, in fact several months all the test subjects were brought back and another MRI scan carried out. The results were interesting, the brain scan for the group who did nothing, well funny enough nothing had changed, the area of the brain affected still showed inactivity, the other test group however showed that the brain had circumvented the area of the brain damaged by the stroke by creating new neural pathways.

Act moment:

What activity have you been putting off from having a go at, is it learning a new language? How about learning how to ride a unicycle? Write down a list of 10 things you would really like to try, then find out how to do the top 3 over the next seven days.

www.alumni.cam.ac.uk/magazine

8. Own

Who owns your thoughts? Who owns your feelings? Oh yes that's right it's you! All too often we allow people to dictate to us how we should be thinking and feeling about things. Let us put a stop to that right now.

There are nearly 7.5 billion people living on this planet and no two people are exactly the same, we are all unique. Yes, there may be similarities, like the colour of our hair or eyes and people have common traits in the way they approach a piece of work and the way in which they do their thinking. The important thing to remember is we are all our own person.

Bob Marley once said 'Every man gotta right to decide his own destiny,' let's not be sexist this is also applicable to women (I digress), he's got something there. There are 4P's in how you deal with life, you can be a 'Prisoner' feeling that you're confined and restricted in what and how you do things. You could be a 'Protester' arguing and shouting about things and saying how unfair life is and how badly you're being treated. Are you more of a 'Passenger' letting someone else make decisions for you and take you along for the ride or are you a 'Participant' someone who engages in discussions and lets people know how you feel, what you're thinking in other words playing an active role in where you're going and how you're going to get there.

Decide to be a 'Participant' take control of what is going on, own your thoughts and feeling. What can you choose to do differently to take more control of your life?

On another note a great gift you can give someone is feedback and I'm not talking 'constructive feedback' because that's just code for 'I'm going to dump on you from a great height' but phrase it in such a way that it sounds like it's going to be helpful. If you are ever going to give feedback, own it! The 'feedback' can come in many forms and often when people even hear the mere mention of the word, internally they go into shutdown. Let's decide to change that, now!

Act moment:

Over the next 7 days look for an opportunity to give someone you know some appreciative feedback letting them know how they made you feel and think about a kind action they either did for you directly or for another person. Ken Blanchard in his book 'The One Minute Manager' described how we should catch people doing something right. Go out and surprise a friend by giving them feedback when you have witnessed them doing a good deed.

Blanchard, Ken & Johnson, Spencer. *The One Minute Manager*. Harper. 2011 (Revised Edition)

9. Awe

Life would be pretty boring if the same thing happened every day, we saw the same people, did the same work, ate the same food and watched the same television programmes. For some people life does feel like this, almost like a hamster on its wheel, going around and around. For most of us though life contains major ups and downs, really exciting, fun, amazing highs and painful, challenging lows. When we are in awe of something or someone it can be either positive, negative or sometimes both.

When asked to describe something we are in awe of we usually describe the positives which is where we will be focussing our and your thoughts in this chapter but the origins of the word 'awe' comes from both positive and negative experiences (think of the similarity to the word 'awful'). We could be in awe of the destructive power of an earthquake or similar natural disaster, is takes us by surprise and instils a sense of fear. But something that is awesome is so much better! Something so much bigger than ourselves, something that can take our breath away.

So what people, places, things or whatever else would have you in a state of awe? Have you visited the pyramids of Giza? Maybe the Grand Canyon? Have you met a famous world leader or a personal hero?

These are sure to create that sense of awe but what can you do to experience this amazing feeling on a more regular basis? If we can create more positive experiences for ourselves then life surely has to be better!

Think back to the time you saw your first true love, what was their name again? I can guarantee you when you think about that person and the first time you saw them; you were in awe of them. So whether it is looking at something for the first time, meeting someone amazing or maybe even creating something yourself awe can be a day-to-day emotion. They key is to take the time to look around you, notice more than you're currently noticing? Have you ever been outside at night, lay back and felt awe at the millions and millions of stars in the universe? Have you ever tried a new food and considered the flavour awesome? Have you seen a puppy playing in the snow for the first time? Ok, so maybe that's more of an aww moment than an awe moment!

So what else might have you in a state of awe? We will give you some other examples of our own here that might inspire you to do more, see more and feel more. After all, we are emotional beings and actively pursuing positive emotions has got to better than slipping into the negative ones. For those interested in the arts what about theatre, ballet, opera, an art gallery or a museum.

Looking at the skeleton of a dinosaur at the National History Museum, watching Swan Lake at the Royal Albert Hall and looking at Constable's The Hay Wain at the National Gallery or even visiting the location that inspired his painting (near Flatford on the river Stour in Suffolk) are a few of our moments. Maybe you will be in awe of your favourite pop or rock band, if so, get yourself some tickets! How about going to watch your favourite sports team? Or even booking that dream holiday that you have always dreamt of!

Act moment:

Over the next week, look for 3 things that you are in awe of. These could be people, places, objects, events or just about anything. The key to recognising them is that they should really make you stop and think, you'll know when you feel that sense of awe. And if you are the kind of person who says "I'll never see anything that amazing this week then it is either time to open your eyes a little wider to the world around you or it's time to go out a little further into the world, maybe visit some new places, meet some new people or take on a new challenge.

Three things that have inspired awe in me are…

1.

2.

3.

10. Wow

What makes you say WOW? What things make you almost have to catch your breath? Could it be a beautifully restored E-type Jaguar majestically driving down the road, an amazing animal you have seen for the first time on the National Geographic channel or other nature programme? A beautiful sunset while you are standing on a sun kissed beach? It could even be something like the opening credits to a new movie you have been waiting to see for months?

Some or all of these could be things that make us go Wow! It might even be the first kiss you had with your partner. Wow moments often leave us speechless, we might even go as far as to say you get a shiver running down your spine or Goosebumps on your arms, making the hairs on the back of your neck stand up as though they have been charged with a jolt of electricity.

We live in an incredibly fast world and more often than not we are head down looking at our phones and watching the latest podcast we downloaded. STOP! Put the device down and step away. How about stepping away for even 30 minutes a day? Look up, take the time to appreciate the wondrous things around us, the sky, nature, the architecture around us.

How does this help us? So what if there are impressive things and people all around us? It's said that "you never really appreciate something until it's gone" so imagine that for a moment. Imagine everything becomes grey in colour, nothing has any sound, everything feels flat, and there are no patterns, no movement, just stillness. Hopefully you're not too depressed thinking about that! Maybe now you might reconsider all the amazing things that could make us say "wow". Maybe it's not just the super-amazing things, maybe ordinary everyday things could make you feel the same? When you're ill you often say "Oh, I just want to feel well again" but when you're well do you truly appreciate it? Try waking up each morning and saying "wow, I feel ok!".

Hmm moment:

Think back to a time when you first experienced these sensations, for some it may be further back than others. Use your imagination, you could either think of yourself like a young child looking around them at everything for the first time with innocence. The other option is this, picture yourself as a person who has had their sight restored, having been blind. How do you look at things? The next part is to buy a journal and yes we are talking an actual journal, not an electronic device, good old pen and paper. For some this will be 'old school'. Start capturing those things that leave you with that 'WOW' factor. What exactly was it about that experience that gave you a 'Wow' feeling?

11. God

Let us clarify something from the start, we are not going to start preaching to or at you. Let us also clarify that we know there are numerous different religious denominations and countless different names given to an entity for whom people believe in. We have used the name 'God' as it fits our 3-letter word criteria. That is the only reason. We are not saying anyone is better or worse than any other, we're not qualified or knowledgeable enough to have that debate or discussion. Our purpose here is to consider the impact that religion, belief or spirituality has had in the past and still today continues to have in many people's lives and learn from it.

We want you to recognise the massive, positive impact that belief, faith and prayer can have on people's lives whether it is people being thankful for what they have got or during times of worry or hardship. You may not consider yourself a religious or spiritual person but you can still adapt or use what others do to help you on your quest for change.

What do religions or belief give us? Spiritual belief is very strong in a large number of people, irrespective of what part of the world they come from so there must be benefits. Life really is a mixture of what we put into it, our energy, efforts and actions plus what the world has in store for us; a certain amount of luck, chance and circumstance.

We can control what we put out into the world but we cannot control what the world gives us. This is where we can have faith that certain things were always meant to be that way, they were beyond our control. We have to be accepting that whatever our efforts or intentions life won't always work out as planned and that is OK. We can get upset, annoyed or stressed but it's much better if we succumb to the bigger picture, the higher power or Mother Nature and accept the world the way it is.

Take a moment to think about something in your life that happened that was totally out of your control. It may be a car accident, an illness or the death of a loved one. These can be major life-changing events. Now take a few moments to sit and think about them. Be aware if you start going down the "if only I had…" or "if only there had been…" routes. These are routes than often lead to blaming yourself, others or circumstances. Say to yourself now "I accept that this was just the way it was". It's ok to be upset or angry or many other emotions but you need to get to a place of acceptance. It was always going to be that way. Acceptance is much better for you than blame or denial.

As well as belief, religion also usually conveys a set of values. With many families now choosing not to engage in religious belief where do children get their values from? Where did you get yours? Family? Friends? Television?

If you have children, instilling a good set of values is probably the most important thing you can do as a parent. If you don't have children, you can still impact others by having good values and staying true to them.

In the Chapter 2, you took time to write out some aims; to have a clear destination for a better life. The end result though is not enough by itself. Staying true to your values while achieving your aims is truly a better way. So what are your values? What behaviours or attributes are really important to you? Here's a few suggestions:

Love, trust, honesty, fun, loyalty, creativity, positivity, passion, respect, health, education, adventure, courage, efficiency, open mindedness, commitment, consistency, care.

Which of these stand out most to you? Consider how these currently show up in your life, are you able to stay true to them in all you do? Another way to understand your values is when other people do things that annoy or upset you. These emotions usually come from someone crossing your values. Know your values and then check that how you live your life is congruent with them.. Many of them are covered in different forms in this book so we hope we're helping.

Let's now look at 'spirituality' from another angle. Spirituality is often associated with and can be satisfied by giving something back and we are not talking solely money.

If you have not got a lot of money, there is something even more precious…. Time! Money can be earned; time is something you never get back. In the 2000 movie 'Pay it Forward' starring Kevin Spacey as one of the main characters, he introduced a very simple idea: Do one random act of kindness for three strangers and the only repayment you accept is that they then do one random for another three strangers and so on, and on. Think about it, how big an impact could we have on the world if everyone was to do this? Unbelievable is a word that springs to my mind. How satisfying would it be, being part of something bigger than ourselves?

Act moment:
Over the next seven days see what random acts of kindness you can offer. Carry shopping bags for an old person, help someone across the road, put a neighbours bin out for them, offer to teach someone a skill you have, volunteer your time for some charity work or go and visit someone who would appreciate it. Yes, three would be great but don't limit yourself.

12. Day

Ok so this may be hard for some to comprehend, but we're going to say it anyhow. There are 365 days a year (excluding leap years of course), 52 weeks, 12 months, 7 days in a week, and 24 hours a day. We all have 24 hours in a day, no matter how rich or poor you might be we all get the same amount of time to play with, each and every one of us. Some of us get more days if we live longer, some of us get less but each day is the same.

The choice then is what you do with each day you have. Do you make each day count? Have you ever wasted a few days? It is not about living some 'perfect' life but it is about understanding the impact on your life if you choose to live your days 'on purpose' and not just 'by accident'. So how then can you do this?

Let us be clear, it's not about time management it's about prioritising. You can't manage time. It just exists. You can prioritise what's most important to you and make choices about what you do and when. When you're at work do you put in your best effort or do you allow yourself to get distracted with meaningless activities? At home, do you laze around all day at the weekend or do you make the most of the time you have with your family?

When out with friends do you engage in stimulating conversation, have a laugh, really listen to each other or are you the one staring at your smartphone waiting for the latest update to excite you? Is watching a video of a cat falling off a table really so much more important to you than your friend? Really?

Each of us has to take greater ownership of our time and not waste it. That's not to say you have to be busy all the time. Making a conscious choice to have a relaxing day can be exactly what you need. Rest and recuperation can often be needed. Ensure it is a conscious choice though.

Read through the following book passage and consider how it makes you feel:

'Imagine there is a bank account that credits your account each morning with £86,400. It carries over no balance from day to day. Every evening the banks deletes whatever part of the balance you failed to use during the day. What would you do? Draw out every penny, of course? Each of us has such a bank. Its name is time. Every morning it credits you with 86,400 seconds. Every night it writes off as lost, whatever of this you have failed to invest to a good purpose. It carries over no balance. It allows no overdraft. Each night it burns the remains of the day. If you fail to use the day's deposits the loss is yours. There is no drawing against 'tomorrow.' You must live in the present on today's deposits.

Levy, Marc. *If Only It Were True*. Fourth Estate. 2000

Invest it so as to get from it the utmost in health, happiness and success. The clock is running. Make the most of today.'

Hopefully that has made you think. If you each received £86,400, how would you invest it? How are you going to make the most of the time you have today?

Is your day going to be spent complaining, moaning and wishing things had turned out better or will you now decide that today IS the day that you've been waiting for to achieve your goals, to live a better life, to dream bigger and bolder than you ever have before? And we're not just talking about positive thinking here, we're talking about action too.

Act moment:
Choosing to take actions each and every day that help you fulfil your dreams. Not one of us can say we don't have a spare 10 minutes a day that we could use to do something like Read a book, write a journal, make that phone call you have been putting off, really look at your financial situation, book that check-up, go for a short run, clean out that drawer or cupboard. There is plenty more you could do. If you keep up this great habit of spending just 10 minutes a day on something really useful, over the year you will have put in over 60 hours!

Now you're used to finding just 10 minutes a day, find 10 more. Don't dive straight into 20 as you may struggle and will get put off early. Stick to 10 then once the habit is ingrained add another 10.

Get used to doing it every day. With 20 minutes a day you're now doing 120 hours a year of meaningful, useful work on you, personal development that isn't theoretical, it's real and you can see and feel the results. Based on a typical working week of 40 hours it's the equivalent of 3 week's personal development a year. Very few people do this much. Do it and you'll be one massive step ahead of the game.

13. Fun

Who enjoys having fun? Hands up!

We all do and on occasions it's at an appropriate time and in other instances, not so much. What does having 'fun' really mean to you? Is your life fun? Or do you live a life of misery, complaining about everything, struggling to get through the day or having the thought of 'I'm bored!' irrespective of what is going on around you? It's been said the 'boring people get bored' so what's the real issue here?

We hate to be the bearers of bad news but the lack of fun in your life is down to just one person... YOU! Then again, and this is the great news, you can do something about it.

Ok, we're realists and life isn't necessarily fun, laughter, joy and smiles every single moment, we all have challenges to deal with, things happen that are out of our control, bosses who just seem to have it in for us and general day to day chores like ironing, cleaning and washing. When and where do you want more fun then?

Work or play? Is your work fun enough? Do you return home feeling relieved that each day is over? STOP a minute. You have 2 choices here. Either do something about it or change jobs.

Yes, you can change your job or career (in fact it's almost expected now that people will have several careers, not just jobs in a lifetime.) but you'll still be the same you wherever you go. Let's work on how you can have fun even in the most serious and boring of jobs. What would an accountant or undertaker do to have fun at work? And why would they want to?

Why have fun at work? It's been proven in numerous studies that people who have more fun at work, work better and stick around longer because they genuinely enjoy being there! So let's get serious… it IS important to have fun at work. The best way to do this is to allow people to be themselves, have pictures, plants, have a space where you can chat and relax. If your workplace doesn't have these kind of things, then get them on the employee suggestion scheme.

The one thing we will give a little warning about here is 'organised fun'. Most employees state that they find the weird and wacky ideas dreamed up by some graduate in the HR department as a 'fun day' anything but fun. Go with what's natural, planned fun usually isn't.

And what about outside of work? Do you have enough fun in your free time? Let's work through some practical examples of how you can have more fun.

1. What's on this weekend? Take a look through the local papers, council internet

sites etc. and see what's going on out there. There's plenty to do ranging from dog shows to air shows, steam fairs to country fairs, art exhibitions to guided walks. Can you honestly say that you know enough about what's going on in and around where you live?

2. Evenings. Summer is lovely, having a few drinks and a barbecue in the garden but what happens when it gets colder? Do you find yourself sat in front of the TV watching the same shows over and over? So, how can you have more fun on those cold winter evenings?

There really are limitless opportunities to add more fun to your life. Here are a few more examples that we or people we know have experienced:

- Move to a new town, city or village - Explore somewhere new and making new friends
- Change your routine - Try a new route to work, talk to new people or eat Pizza for breakfast!
- Plan a secret party or weekend away - surprise someone you care about
- Do whatever your friends don't expect you to do
- Watch something funny - this could be a live comedian a comedy TV programme or some amazing clips on YouTube
- Go and test-drive a sports car - fun when you know you don't have to buy it but still get to drive it!

- Get creative - paint, draw, design, create or make. As long as you enjoy it.

So there's just a few ideas. They may or may not be right for you but the choice is out there just waiting for you.

Act moment:

Today do at least one thing that you consider fun or turn an activity that you would normally consider 'boring' into a fun activity. If painting your kitchen is boring, invite some friends round for a kitchen painting party and supply them with food and drink. It'll be cheaper than hiring professionals and much more fun than doing it by yourself. A happy medium!

14. Ask

Who are the best people at asking questions? That's right, children. They are phenomenal at asking questions because their minds are like sponges thirsty for knowledge, granted though the question they ask the most, is normally 'Why?'. They want a deeper understanding of the world and the way it works.

Actually, we are ALL great at asking questions because we were all once very young and we wanted to understand the world in which we live in. The challenge comes as we get older we often get told to 'lose some of that curiousness and become more accepting of 'that's just the way it is'. Well we don't like that style of thinking. We believe the more questions the better. Just imagine if James Dyson had never asked "How can we make a carpet cleaner that doesn't lose suction?" or Steven Spielberg had never asked "How can we make people like this E.T. character?" Great questions demand great answers.

If that is true then our aim is to help you ask more, better questions. Here are a few questions that we know can make a real difference:

Getting other people to like you

Many people enjoy a trip to the hairdresser or barber. Why? Because when sitting in that chair you are guaranteed to be asked questions. Yes, some will be cliché such as "Going away anywhere nice this year" but at least (assuming they are genuinely interested) they are making the conversation about you. And we all know the most important person from our own perspective - ourselves! What we all need to do is to start asking not only more questions, but better questions. We need to be more interested in others as this will give us a better understanding of them and will undoubtedly lead to a better relationship.

By better questions we mean questions that will stop people in their tracks. Ask questions like why? How? Who? If you already ask lots of questions, then fantastic; keeping asking them. If you don't then start! Be curious. Be interested in others and not just so you can then boast that your life, car, house or bank statement is better than theirs. Keep the focus on them and you'll find they like you a lot more.

Getting what you want from life

Think for a minute what you can ask for: A pay rise. Your steak to be cooked the way you like it. Someone to marry you. A discount. Help. If you don't ask you'll never know. Also, you can ask yourself "How can I improve my life?" or "How can I afford that Porsche I've always wanted?" or "How will I know when I've got the life I want?"

These kind of questions really get our brains active and are so much better than simply complaining that life is no good.

Asking for help
Not everyone has all the answers so if you need help or support with something then ask. Some people believe asking for help is a sign of weakness. The reality is, it's not. Asking for help takes bravery because it shows a vulnerability and people appreciate that. There are many experts out there and you don't have to struggle alone. Why take all that time to redesign the wheel when you can ask someone else who has already designed it.

Act moment:
Be curious listen to questions other people ask, think about them and if need be write them down, or record them in a journal. Have a list of 'my favourite questions' and add to it regularly. You'll soon become a master questioner. And if you need a little more help then watch a few chat shows. Hosts like Jonathan Ross or Piers Morgan have different styles but both know how to ask a great question.

15. See

Assuming you don't walk around with your eyes closed every day then your eyes see a huge amount. As well as real life we now have smartphones so that every minute of the day we have something to feast our eyes upon. But with so much to contend with, how much do we really 'see'. Do you stop and really look at things and people? As mentioned earlier in the book the majority of people have 5 sensory preferences with which we take in information, visual being the most prevalent. So how do we make use of what we see to improve our lives?

Ok, pause for just a moment. Look around you and take a few minutes to see what you've previously not seen. Really study the room or place you are in. Describe to yourself (or out loud if you prefer) the colours, shapes and textures that you can see. How light or dim is it? What's the same as it was the last time you were here? What's changed, moved or is different?

Did you notice anything you've not noticed before? Often when we really stop to look we see things that we've 'seen' before but never really noticed. Has someone you know ever changed their hairstyle or bought new clothes and then got upset because you never noticed? That's an immediate improvement you can make!

Really start to take in the appearance of others. When you get good at this, move on from physical appearance i.e. clothes, hair, jewellery etc. to facial expressions. Really notice how people look when they are happy or sad, free or frustrated. The more you pick up the better you'll be at connecting with other people and understanding how they are feeling or when something is not quite right.

Now for a different perspective. Pick any object you can see from where you are now. Imagine zooming in 100 times closer, maybe even a 1000. What would it look like? Just using your imagination, you can create a different visual picture in your mind. Now imagine zooming out. What would where you are now look like from 10 miles or 100 miles up?

So 'seeing' can be what you can actually see but also what you can visualise. Some people create helpful visualisations, 'seeing the best' in people or situations while others tend to create an image that wasn't actually completely true. One great story we heard was of a bride who at the end of her big day spilled red wine over her dress. When asked later about her day she visualised herself wearing the wine stained dress throughout the entire day! Imagine then how she felt about her wedding day. So check your memories are true and not an unhelpful image!

Many, if not all of the world's greatest sports people visualise themselves winning the competition whether it's a boxing match, an athletic sport or a formula one race.

They see themselves as champions. They also, very importantly visualise themselves doing the necessary practice, putting in the effort and going through all the challenges they know that are required along the way. So how do you see yourself?

Another thing to consider is the phrase 'seeing is believing'. Do you believe everything you see? When you watch the news or read a newspaper do believe that it is true? Do you believe that it is completely neutral and unbiased? Remember, even those reporting the news do so from their own perspective. Be aware that your perspective is influenced by that of others.

Hmm moment:
Close your eyes and imagine looking in a mirror. Now describe yourself! Not just in terms of physical attributes (although do notice whether you focus on the attributes you are most or least happy with) but also describe the personality you see i.e. "I see someone who's strong, committed to improving the lives of their families and for themselves. I see someone who knows what they want and will do whatever it takes to achieve it"

Notice what you 'see' that you're not so happy about too. Which of these attributes that you've identified would, if improved, have the biggest impact on your life?

Great, now you can really see where you're going! As the phrase goes, seeing is believing so start off by seeing what you want in your mind's eye and most importantly, visualise what you need to do to change it and then you're more likely to see it for real.

16. Gig

We have never met anyone yet who doesn't like music. Granted we may all have different tastes but there is something in music that seems to go deeper than logic or emotion, it goes deep into the soul of every human being. Music appears to have the power to make us happy or sad, it can get us motivated, or even dancing round the kitchen. Couples have 'our song', teams and countries have anthems, and many of us have a song that we feel talks directly to us or somehow seems to explain key moments in our lives. So how do we use this for the better?

Okay so let us give you 3 small challenges which you will enjoy:

Challenge 1: Learn the lyrics. Have you ever noticed that with some of your favourite songs you know most of the lyrics, definitely the chorus but there's a few you make up along the way? Well now is the time to learn them, properly. A simple challenge maybe but you will feel great once you know them 100%, in fact the next time you hear it sing along.

Challenge 2: Try new music. Like many things in life our music can be force of habit. We find certain artists we like or a particular radio station and we stick to it. Every so often try changing to a random new station.

Notice the music, what do you like? What is different about the DJ's? Notice how it feels to be doing something that you would not normally consider yourself doing. Step a little outside your comfort zone. Put your headphones on at work and listen to some classical music and notice how you feel about telling your colleagues "Oh yeah, I'm listening to Bach!". Fulfilling a similar challenge, I once went to HMV and purchased a CD from an artist I had never even heard of before to ensure I really was trying something new. OK, it's not now in my top 10 favourites list but I did find a few tracks I really liked. Now we live in the world of downloads and streaming this is even easier to do. Try some new music today.

Challenge 3: Let's Dance! Music is not just about listening... It is also about dancing. If you are now thinking "I can't dance though" then have a read of Chapter 5 again about limiting beliefs. Remember everyone can move their body, some better than others and that is fine! Music can and does have a positive effect.

Hmm moment:

When you need inspiration or motivation what type of music would you listen to? Research has proven that when exercising the right music can help us work out harder and for longer. It has also been shown that faster music makes us drive faster so do also keep an eye on those speed limits when you're next listening to some beats.

17. Gym

Be honest now, were you tempted to skip straight to the next chapter when you read the word 'gym'? Or are you someone who already goes and knows the benefits? A gym is a bit like Marmite, people often say that you either love or hate it. But is that a fixed mindset we spot?

Yes, some do love it and you will find them there 6 days a week. Others you will see there every so often following the same routine and never really improving their fitness or physique. Some you will hear at work complaining that "Oh, I've got to go to the gym" and probably finding whatever excuse they can not to go, others will say "I don't want to go because I don't want to be 'musclebound'" - do they really think it's that easy to pack on a huge amount of muscle? It is just another way of saying "I don't want to go". There are many other excuses and reasons not to go from "I just don't have the time" to "It's just full of posers," to "I really couldn't be bothered."

So, what is our advice? Well firstly we are going to recommend going to the gym. Then secondly we are going to recommend not going. So this chapter IS for everyone!

Why you should go to the gym: The human body has not yet adapted to sitting in front of a PC all day or sitting behind the wheel of a car for 5 hours straight.

Your body needs to be up and about, moving and working to burn off calories. If your job is not a physical one, then you need to exercise. Diet industries generate billions of pounds a year helping people create the 'perfect look.' Who though defines what perfect is? Your aim is your choice. The key then to achieving their aim for some people can be as simple as eat less, move more. The gym is the right place for this exercise as you can exercise any muscle you want, and complete either aerobic (anything that gets you breathing heavily such as running, swimming, rowing or cycling) or anaerobic exercise (lifting and moving heavy objects slowly to challenge the muscles) to burn calories and improve your strength, tone, and health.

The other major benefit of the gym is not physical, it is mental. Your brain and body are interconnected and exercise has been shown to increase mental performance, reduce stress and improve your sleep which in turn has a massively positive impact on you.

Here are our top ten considerations if you are contemplating finding and going to a gym:

1. Visit 3-5 gyms before signing up. In some you will feel more at home at than others. You need to find a place that you feel comfortable in.
2. Classes or Individual exercise; which would you prefer? Some people are more social and like to work out as part of a friendly

group. Some just like to be left alone to get on with it.

3. What else is on offer there? Do they offer team sports, or swimming? Do they have a Physiotherapist on site? What will you enjoy or what will benefit you most?

4. Are the facilities what you expect? Cold changing rooms with dirty showers can be enough to demotivate you from going.

5. Food. Many gyms now offer food and drink (hopefully healthy!) for after your workout. What a great reward for your workout as well as replacing the protein you need for your muscles. Also, don't go to the gym unless you are prepared to look at your diet too.

6. Set goals. Don't even think about attending unless you have a goal. Many people have a New Year's resolution to 'get fit' without a clue as to what 'fit' actually means to them (which is why we have gone for 'gym' rather than 'fit'). Here are some of our different challenges that may be included in your 'fitness':
    - Strength - Can your muscles cope with what's required of them?
    - Flexibility - Not something you really appreciate until you haven't got any.
    - Stamina - How long can you keep going when you need to? Are you ready to run for that bus?

7. Make going to the gym part of your daily routine, either before or after work. Plan ahead when you will attend and stick to the plan. Decide which days fit your life best.

Remember, tomorrow never comes so "Oh I'll go tomorrow" is usually an 'I'm not going.'

8. Can you use it enough? Many gyms charge a monthly fee no matter how often you attend. This is great value if you go regularly but if your sessions are less regular then you may benefit from using a site like payasugym.com where you can pay by the session, week or month.
9. Travelling a lot? Many gyms are part of chains and will let you use their gyms across the country so no excuse not to go while you are away working. Find out which other gyms you can visit. Alternatively, only stay in hotels that have an on-site gym. Sometimes the variety is also motivational.
10. Find friends who go. Just be careful to find friends that help rather than hinder you. A good gym friend should encourage you to go in the first place and then support you in achieving your goals, not spending 45 minutes of your hour there chatting to you about their how their sister is struggling financially because their cat got run over and they couldn't afford the expensive vet's bill... blah blah blah!

Don't go to the gym. Yes, as we said we will now advise you not to go to the gym. We realise that it is not for everyone, although we are all welcome to give it a go. As long as you are getting enough physical exercise then why pay to move weights that don't need moving?

Here are ten physical exercises that avoid you needing to go to a gym:

1. Gardening - Have you even grown your own vegetables? If you have no garden that's alright what about getting an allotment or even helping with a neighbours or relative's garden instead. Mowing the lawn burns 250-350 calories per hour!
2. Walking - This could be either by yourself or with a local club. You might even want to take a dog with you. If not your own maybe an elderly neighbours dog or find a local animal sanctuary or rescue shelter that could do with your support
3. Running or jogging - Work out what distance you want to achieve over what time period, then get outside, totally free of charge. The only thing you will want to invest in is a good pair of trainers and maybe some high visibility clothing
4. Swimming - When was the last time you visited your local swimming pool? Does it have a swimming club you could join? This really is great low impact exercise.
5. Painting and decorating or other DIY - This really depends on how big a job you want to undertake. Start smaller, building up your skill-set before moving on to building a two storey extension
6. Rock climbing - This could of course be either an internal or external venue. There are hundreds of indoor climbing walls across the UK.

7. Joining a team sport - Maybe you are more of a social being and enjoy the camaraderie of playing alongside team mates. How about a sport like football, rugby, netball, hockey, basketball or volleyball?
8. Cycling - Which preference do you have? Would you prefer mountain biking over rough terrain or do you prefer to ride a road bike? Go online and find out which cycling clubs are near you.
9. Canoeing or Rowing - Getting out on a river or local outdoor pursuits centre or for the more adventurous and experienced people how would you like to do some white water?
10. Horse Riding - Either in a Riding school or going on a trekking holiday.

We know there are plenty more activities out there, so go give up that gym membership that you are paying for and not using! If these non-gym activities seem more your kind of thing, then a great site we would recommend is goodgym.org. It is a site where people get together to exercise by doing good. What a fantastic idea.

Hmm moment:

Decide now how you will get enough exercise. To gym or not to gym, that is the question. And enjoy your exercise whether at the gym or not, just make sure you do it.

Irrespective of what you decide to do, please always:

1. Take the advice from the experts, when using equipment for the first time and
2. If you venture into the 'non gym' activities go to authorised locations and business who have been trained and are appropriately insured.

18. Nap

Catching some Zzz's can make such a difference. Albert Einstein is renowned for having naps rather than a full night's sleep and look what he achieved. We are not condoning this if you are a long distance lorry driver or someone who is responsible for operating heavy machinery. Research has shown that a 20 to 30-minute cat nap can be beneficial in improving your short term alertness and performance.

A study at NASA on sleepy military pilots and astronauts found that a 40-minute nap improved performance by 34% and alertness 100%. Take a look at babies, they nap whenever they need to and then have the energy to scream all day! Many other animals nap regularly too so it's not unusual. Sleep experts also recommend that if you feel drowsy when driving, you should immediately pull over to a rest area, drink a caffeinated beverage and take a 20-minute nap. Don't go over 30 minutes though or you will probably wake feeling quite groggy.

As well as napping, understanding how to get a full night's sleep and rest is essential. We say 'rest' as well as 'sleep' because have you ever slept all night but then woken feeling even more tired than you did when you first went to bed? Us too.

Here are five top tips to being really rested at night:

a) Switch off. For at least 30 minutes before bed switch off your TV and have a conversation. As well as allowing your brain to switch off from the bombardment of images you can discuss and 'put to bed' thoughts whizzing through your mind. Switch off you email too. Reading that 'ultra-important' email from your boss at 10:30pm can have you thinking it over all night.

b) Limit your food/drink. Even though it can feel like alcohol helps you get to sleep, it really reduces the quality of your sleep. And quality is equally important if not more important than quantity. Eating too late will mean your body is busy working to digest the food while you're trying to nod off. Don't have caffeine too late in the day too as this can keep some people awake.

c) Follow your body's natural rhythms but aiming to go to bed around the same time each night, not laying in until different times each morning and not falling asleep on the sofa after dinner - instead get up and do things that will keep you away until bedtime.

d) Check your mattress and pillows. When was the last time you changed them? Comfort and support are essential to a good night's sleep. Here's a simple way to test your pillows. With the pillowcase removed, fold the pillow in half and put it on the floor. Now put a pair of trainers on it (clean ones preferably!). If the pillow is in good condition it will spring open and flip the trainers off. If it's too old, it will just sit there. Go and try now!

e) Be cool. Check your room temperature. Yes, some of us prefer to feel warm at night but the best sleep is not when you are too hot. If you can, open a window and get some fresh air circulating around the room.

Act moment:

Write yourself a 'sleep plan'. What are you going to do or change this week to improve the quality of sleep you have? Include in your plan whether or not you'll benefit from the occasional nap and where and when you can have it.

19. Eat

Feeling great and healthy is a combination of mental health and physical health. Physically we can move our bodies (see Chapter 17 - Gym) and get enough sleep (Chapter 18 - Nap) then all we need to do to complete the triangle is to eat well. All three work together to form our physical health. There is a cross-over however as mental health such as stress levels can also have a negative impact on your physical health.

So what does food mean to you? Is it fuel to give you enough energy? Is it for comfort? Is it a luxury? Is it just something that you have never really considered before? Take a moment to consider your relationship with food. Do you actively choose what is right for you or are you following old, maybe less helpful habits? Do you remember when your parents told you to "always clear your plate"?

Even though they had good intentions at the time of not wasting food, that attitude now can be really unhelpful in this day and age as more often than not food is in abundance and readily accessible. For goodness sake, from the comfort of your own home you can sit on your sofa, order a complete meal and have it delivered to your door. My local kebab shop offers a 'meal for one' which consists of a kebab, a pizza, wedges and 2 cans of fizzy drink!! Finishing a plateful of that is way more than anyone needs unless they are exercising 6 hours a day.

And what do you think about the word 'diet'? Suffering withdrawal symptoms from all your favourite foods? Tiny meals? Salad? Just the thought can have you reaching for a hamburger! Our advice is never to 'diet' what comes off can go back on just as quickly. Make the decision now to make permanent changes to your eating habits remember 'I am what I eat.' Eating healthy means being healthy, eating crap (not literally) makes you feel crap! Clear enough? Sorry to be so blunt but that's the way it is.

What should you eat? How much? When should you eat it? These are all great questions that experts over time have challenged one another on and change over time depending on current research findings. Fat was bad. Then it was sugar. Now certain fats are good for you! Three meals a day? Or should it be Two? Or maybe five? Do I snack or wait, which is better? Big breakfast or big dinner? Confusing right? If this area interests you then please do more research, find new recipes that look and sound appealing, try new foods and conduct your own personal food experiments. After all, as much as we are 99% the same we do know that some bodies react differently to food. There really is no 'one size fits all' magic diet that works for everyone. Make small changes, give it time and notice the results. Are you getting fatter or slimmer? Are you feeling more or less energised? Are you regularly hungry or do you regularly feel stuffed? Learn about your own body, that is the best way forward.

The key element to this is recognising patterns. Do you have a sugar craving mid-afternoon and reach for that bar of chocolate? Or maybe after your evening meal? Once you recognise 'when' you are eating less helpful food then you can plan the alternative and eat something more nutritious and healthy. Take a banana or an apple to work ready for that mid-afternoon craving or find a healthy dessert that you can have after dinner. Just because something say reduced rate does not mean you eat two of them. Be prepared rather than trying to just cut it out or ignore the feeling as this generally doesn't work.

Now here's probably our most important advice: Healthy eating starts long before meal time. Most people if they have chocolate, crisps and a bottle of wine in the house will consume them. Not surprisingly if they leave them in the shop, they won't. Take time now to consider your shopping habits, what do you plan to buy? Healthy eating can only start with healthy buying. If it is not on your shopping list don't buy. Did you know supermarkets place the healthy fruit and vegetables at the front of the store so that you will feel so virtuous about buying healthy food that you then allow yourself some 'treats' as rewards as you continue your shop? They know that if they put all the chocolate and crisps in the first aisle then you would be more likely to whizz past them as quick as you can to get your shopping done and out of there. Do not fall foul of their sales techniques! Stick to your list and be strong.

http://www.mindbodygreen.com/wc/abby-phon

Act moment:

For the next week keep a food journal of everything you eat and drink. Yes, that includes the sneaky can of drink or packet of sweets as there's a lot of calories in those too. And make sure you include 'when' you eat and drink, not just what. At the end of the week look over the journal and consider what is helping and what is hindering you. This is an important first step. Only from here can you start to plan your changes.

20. Sip

This chapter leads on really nicely from Chapter 19, Eat. Our bodies are made up of between 60-70% water, therefore to function properly we need to keep it hydrated. We know this might come across a little crude, what colour is your pee? If it's Berocca orange, that can mean one of 2 things:

1. You have recently had a Berocca and it's worked its way through your system or
2. You are dehydrated and you are not drinking enough water.

Research has shown that drinking at least 2 litres of water a day can have real benefits. From an article by Abby Phon in Mind Body Green (20th March 2012) she discusses a number of benefits to drinking more water, including:
1. Increases Energy & Relieves Fatigue: Since your brain is mostly water, drinking it helps you think, focus and concentrate better and be more alert. As an added bonus, your energy levels are also boosted!
2. Promotes Weight Loss: Removes by-products of fat, reduces eating intake (by filling up your stomach if consumed prior to meals), reduces hunger (hello natural appetite suppressant!), raises your metabolism and has zero calories!
3. Flushes Out Toxins: Gets rid of waste through sweat and urination which reduces

the risk of kidney stones and UTI's (urinary tract infections).

4. Improves Skin Complexion: Moisturizes your skin, keeps it fresh, soft, glowing and smooth. Gets rid of wrinkles. It's the best anti-aging treatment around!
5. Maintains Regularity: Aids in digestion as water is essential to digest your food and prevents constipation.
6. Boosts Immune System: A water guzzler is less likely to get sick. And who wouldn't rather feel healthy the majority of the time? Drinking plenty of water helps fight against flu, cancer and other ailments like heart attacks.
7. Natural Headache Remedy: Helps relieve and prevent headaches (migraines & back pains too!) which are commonly caused by dehydration.
8. Prevents Cramps & Sprains: Proper hydration helps keep joints lubricated and muscles more elastic so joint pain is less likely.

Other research has shown that it can also help with long term memory.

How much tea or coffee do you drink? Excessive amounts of caffeine can also be bad for you. We are not saying you need to stop drinking your tea or coffee that is not our place, what we are saying is it's alright within reason, you are still taking liquid into your body.

Depending on which website or research paper you read having a glass of wine can have benefits, on the other hand a bottle a night would have the opposite effect. The best thing to remember is everything in moderation. You need liquid entering your body to keep you hydrated. When you look at a large bottle of water, you might say to yourself there is no way I'm going to finish all that.

Act moment:
Carry around a water bottle with you, around 500 - 750ml in size. This size of a bottle works better for several reasons, firstly it should fit with relative ease into most bags, secondly often when we are presented with what looks like a big task in our minds we say, 'no way, I can't do it.' By using a smaller bottle, it breaks the task down into a more achievable chunks. Remember to drink and refill 3 to 4 times a day and record how you feel in the journal we discussed in 'Eat.'

21. Air

Breathing. You have already got this, right? In, out, in and out again. Sorted!

Think about this for a moment though. Surviving without food, you could last between 7-10 days at a push, without water around 2-3 days. Yet see how long you last not breathing, you would only last minutes. Breathing air is essential, you have a greater need than food & water. Air affects you both physically and mentally as it is providing oxygen to your brain and body and we do it all the time, but are we making the most of it? Do you really get enough oxygen to perform at your best? You may notice more if your work involves you sitting in a chair for long periods of time, if you slouch over and your posture is not great then you really aren't breathing at your best.

We will give you a number of useful suggestions in this chapter of the book on how to improve the quality and quantity of air you are breathing so that you can really get the best from your body physically and mentally and we will start this with a simple test. Ready?

Find yourself some space and lay down on the floor, on your back. Place one hand on your chest and the other on your stomach. Now relax and just breathe. Notice which hand rises and falls as you breathe in and out. Is it the hand on your chest or on your stomach?

If it is the one on your chest try keeping it still and allow your breath to go right into your stomach. If you are already breathing and your stomach is rising more, great keep going. Why is this important? You may have noticed that babies breathe deep down to their stomachs, not just into their chests like many of us do. This is how we naturally breathe as it increases the oxygen we receive and helps us feel calm. When our breathing is high in our chest it is shallower, and much less effective. Have you ever noticed this particularly when you are stressed, nervous or anxious? This is why people will often tell you to "take a few deep breaths, in through your nose. Out through your mouth". The key is learning to do this more often so that we get back to our more natural state of breathing.

We would recommend you practicing this, laying on the floor regularly to check and improve your breathing. You can also improve your breathing through exercise, yoga or other relaxation or breathing techniques such as Qigong or Tai Chi. Maybe you incorporate one of these into your 'non-gym' activities. Why not go to a class and receive expert tuition or if you want to practice now take a look through YouTube where you will find lots of video examples.

If the majority of your day is sitting in a chair at work we would recommend taking regular breaks, ideally go for a walk or if you can find a quiet space do a few stretches while breathing deeply. You will soon notice how much more energy you have throughout the day.

Breathing more effectively can also have a massive impact on your ability to maximise the impact of your exercise. Many people hold their breath when lifting weights, they are normally the ones at the gym with the red faces! The key is to exercise at normal breathing rate, you breathe out as you move (push or pull) the weight and breathe in as you return the weight to its starting position. If you are exercising too fast and breathe at that rate you will be out of breath after each set or if you hold your breath then your muscles will struggle due to insufficient oxygen. Exercising at breathing rate will ensure you are putting sufficient stress onto the muscles and helping them grow and adapt.

Should you ever find yourself having to present to a large audience (which is a huge fear for many people) then using one of these breathing techniques will help you relax, which in turn can make all the difference. Alternatively, if you don't want to be calm and relaxed but really want to go on stage pumped up and energised then taking some much deeper breaths in and out, gradually increasing over 8-10 breaths can really fill you with oxygen and make you want to spring into action!

Hmm moment:
Think out how improving your breathing could improve your life. What would you want from it? Better exercise, more calmness, increased focus, more energy? And if you had one of these, what knock-on effect would that have in your life? And how would that make a difference to you and those around you?

22. Sit

Are you sat down whilst reading this book? If you are then freeze! Stay completely still and take a moment to notice your posture. Are you slouched or upright? Leaning to one side or asymmetric? How long have you been where you are right now? 10 minutes? 3 hours? We all spend more time sitting than is probably good for us as many jobs require us to do so, whether that is in the office, travelling in the car or by train and then when at home, watching TV or doing even more work. It's been said that over 3 hours sitting is incredibly bad for you for a number of reasons.

What is the answer? We would love to say "stop watching TV" but hey, we are realistic, there is some good stuff on there. When watching TV, ensure your back is properly supported and get up every so often for a stretch. What about when you are at work? Every workplace should conduct a workstation assessment where they check that you have the seat and desk you need and if necessary provide you with extra lumbar support, if needed.

If working from home on a laptop, the worst thing you can do is actually have it on your lap! Yes, that's what it was designed for and how it was named but the real problem here is that your neck is bent forward and that can cause spinal problems. Buy yourself a laptop holder or get a desk and work there, ideally with the screen directly in front of your eyes.

You might even like to experiment sitting on one of those bouncy gym balls rather than on a chair, yes some people we know do actually use these!

Now that we've said how sitting can be bad for you let's consider the positive effects of sitting and watching the world go by.

Is your life lived at 100 miles per hour? Do you need to take your foot off the accelerator? When was the last time you switched off? How good are you at relaxing, we mean truly relaxing? If you struggle to really switch off then here's something we'd like you to try: Go to your local coffee shop or a restaurant, sit back and watch what is happening around you. See how people interact with one another; their smiles, greetings and conversations. Look at how people move, how they stand and you will see right in front of your very eyes there's a whole big diverse and interesting world out there.

To truly get away from your own thoughts and feelings and really switch off, pick a person, anyone you see around you (but not someone you know too well) and take 5 minutes really imagining what it's like to be them, what their life is like, what job they do, what hobbies and interests they have. Of course all this is just guess work but for a few minutes you'll find yourself sitting and really switching off.

All too often miss things that happen around us because we are so consumed with what is going on in our own little bubble of a world. Switch off your phone, your kindle or your tablet, sit up straight and look around, enjoy the moment. Just sit and take it all in.

Hmm moment:

Over the next 7 days we recommend some appreciative inquiry and we can guarantee you, you might surprise yourself. Appreciative inquiry is adjusting your focus to the positives and asking questions which direct your thinking in a different way to how many of us currently think. If you're currently asking "what's wrong with my life?" or "what are the problems, I need to fix?" then your mind is direct towards 'wrong' and 'problems'. Try instead asking "what's going well for me right now?" or "what might be the best thing I could achieve today?" This is not burying your head in the sand or ignoring problems but bringing your thinking to a more balanced view.

The best way to do this is to step back from your technology (leave it at home), go sit in a coffee shop with a journal and write down the things that are going well in your life right now. What have been the things you have really appreciated from the last 3 - 6 months?

23. Who

Imagine you suddenly needed help. Who would you pick up the phone to and call? Family or Friends? Who would come through for you when you needed them, even in the middle of the night? We may have hundreds if not thousands of 'friends' on Facebook but how many of them are truly your friends? How many can you rely on or trust? Do you see these people regularly enough? With social media it is very easy to stay in touch, but just looking at someone's latest holiday snaps or pictures of their new-born baby is nothing compared to meeting up in person and hearing them describe the beautiful sandy beaches and lively nightlife or holding their baby in your arms. When was the last time you spent quality time with those that you really do care about?

Who you include in your plans is as important as who you omit. Yes, that may seem harsh but we are here to tell you that some of your 'friends' might be holding you back. It has been said that 'Look at who someone surrounds themselves with and I'll show you the person in 5 years' time,' which we believe to be true. Surround yourself with negative people and you will soon find yourself complaining about this and that and believing that you can't live a better life, you can't get a better job, you can't find that man or woman of your dreams. How about this, choose to spend time with positive people, those that will push you, will challenge you and hold you to your word. What a difference that will make.

Alright we are not saying to suddenly drop all your friends and go seek some more but we are saying to consider how much time you spend with each of these people and what you might want to talk to them about. Would you ask career advice from someone who has stayed in the same job their entire life? Would you ask relationship advice from someone who's been divorced 5 times? Maybe, maybe not!

We would also strongly recommend giving recognition to those who have had a positive impact on you. Have you told the people who have had a major impact on your life what they did and how it affected you? Probably not. If you want to see a great example of this the take a look at the TED talk by Drew Dudley called 'Everyday leadership'.

It's not just about your family and friends. Who are the experts out there who have achieved what you want? What can you learn from them? It's great if you can meet them but if you can't then we'd recommend attending seminars or reading about them. Most really successful people have had books written about them. Learn from the masters.

Hmm moment
Who can you speak to within the next 7 days that will make a positive difference to you? Think which people you really want in your life from now on and how you can spend more time with them.

https://www.ted.com/talks/drew_dudley_everyday_leadership

24. Why

What is the number one question children like to ask? That's right it is, why? As they grow up trying to make sense of the world they are constantly asking the question "why?" Why is the sea blue? Why do I have to go to school? Why is food that tastes so good, so bad for me? And many more besides!

Why is a fantastic question because it asks for meaning, reason, motivation or explanation? It's how we truly understand people and things, well pretty much everything!

The downside. Yes, developing a greater understanding of the world around us can help, but it can also be a hindrance. If you stop to question everything you will probably get very little done and you might annoy one or two people around you. Take a look around your environment right now. This might be your car (please do keep an eye on the road though), your home or your place of work. Why is it the colour it is? Why are things the shape they are? Why is it such as mess? So many questions that you could ask but would also be unnecessary.

Here is a great use of the word 'why' and it's to help solving problems. There is a famous technique from the 1930's which in more recent years was used by Toyota known as the '5-whys' which helps people get to the root cause of a problem.

http://www.toyota-global.com/company/toyota_traditions/quality/mar_apr_2006.html

Let's take a look at a quick example:

Problem: Your client is refusing to pay for the leaflets you printed for them.

1. Why? The delivery was late, so the leaflets couldn't be used.
2. Why? The job took longer than we anticipated.
3. Why? We ran out of printer ink.
4. Why? The ink was all used up on a big, last-minute order.
5. Why? We didn't have enough in stock, and we couldn't order it in quickly enough.

Solution: We need to find a supplier who can deliver ink at very short notice.

As you will see in this example, by asking the 5 why's we have found the root cause of the problem and can decide upon a solution. If we hadn't done this, we may have just thought that the client was being awkward and decided not to work with them again or that our printer was too slow and bought a newer model but neither of these would have resolved the real issue.

How can you use this in your personal life? Here is another more personal example:
Q. Why don't I exercise often enough?
A. Because I regularly work late.
Q. Why do I work late?
A. Because my boss sets unrealistic expectations on me.

Q. Why does he do that?
A. Because he doesn't know that other departments hold me up.
Q. Why doesn't he know?
A. Because I haven't told him.

Solution: Tell your boss about the challenges you are having with the other departments, develop and agree a plan. Now you can get to the gym after work!

Watch out, be careful asking a 'why' question too early on in a conversation because depending on how it's said it can sound threatening. You could even switch it to "What made you take that decision / course of action?" or soften it by saying "I'm really curious as to why you decided to do that?"

Why do you want to achieve the goal? If your 'why' is strong enough then you'll find a way.
A technique we have used in the past to help us position a conversation was to use something called the '4MAT' first created by Bernice McCarthy. The idea is to ask yourself the following questions: Why? What? How? What if...?

Hmm moment:
Use the 5-why's technique on a personal problem or challenge you have. You may need less than 5 or you may need more but generally speaking 5 is enough. Be careful though that the solution you choose is within your control or influence.

http://www.4mat.eu/method-learning-styles.aspx

25. Pet

Yes, we're talking about getting a dog or cat. An owl or pig would be pushing it a bit too far and we would not recommend it. Let us do the disclaimer here first, having a pet is not right for everyone. You may not have the time, money or space for a pet but there are some alternatives which you will find below.

So why have a pet? Well there are approximately 8.5 million dogs and 7.4 million cats in the UK so there really must be some good reasons. Consider the cat or dog first. By looking after them you can be giving them a decent life, a safe home and lots of care and attention which they undoubtedly need and enjoy. And for you, there are many benefits too.

Research shows level of stress drop when stroking a dog. In a survey, many owners said that spending time with their dog leaves them feeling more relaxed, more optimistic and less preoccupied with everyday worries, so when you get home from a stressful day at work it is far better to reach for the dog than a glass of wine or the TV remote control. It is also amazing to feel the unconditional love that a cat or dog offers you. They are always pleased to see you when you get home.

We know that 30-60 minutes of brisk walking a day keeps our hearts much healthier and burns off that dessert you had but without a dog how often will you go for a random walk?

A dog needs walking every day so it's a great motivation to get you outdoors in the fresh air doing a bit of exercise. Be warned, it really is lovely in the summer but not so nice when raining and windy but hey, you will be out there no matter what.

A dog is also great for improving your social life. When out walking, dog owners always get talking to other dog owners and often you will know the dog's name long before you know the owner's! If you have a puppy almost anyone and everyone will stop you in the street and say hi! Taking your dog to puppy training you will not only socialise your dog (very important) but you will also meet others who have the same fun and challenges that you have... you know that a puppy won't wear a nappy right?!

There are other benefits for your family too. There is research proving that babies who grow up in an environment with pets are less likely to have allergies and asthma, and fewer colds and ear infections. Plus, it's great to teach your child/children about caring for animals, not just themselves.

OK, so maybe we've convinced you. If you are now keen to get a cat or dog, then please consider the following points. Having a pet needs an investment, not only financially (food, toys, vet's fees, insurance and furniture if you get a higher maintenance one) you also need to invest time.

For those of you who having a cat or dog right now is not something that will work, here are a few alternatives that you could consider. Not all will give you all the same benefits but small steps in a good direction are better than standing still.

If you like the idea of taking care of a dog, then consider finding a local rescue shelter and help out. Many will let you walk the dogs for them. And if you can't have a pet yourself then maybe donate to the RSPCA, Dogs Trust or Battersea Cats and Dogs home. Maybe even go to a local donkey sanctuary and help out if that's your thing! You could consider having a fish tank as a great alternative, it is very calming to watch them swimming around and you will still have the responsibility or looking after them, feeding them and keeping their tank clean. So there are a few more ideas for you.

Hmm moment:
What would be your number one reason for getting a pet? How much would it change your life? If you already have pets how could you help other people who don't have pets? Taking your dog to visit an elderly relative who can no longer look after one is an amazing thing to do.

26. Fix

We really do live in a disposable society today. If something we own stops working properly, has some minor damage or is starting to fall apart we are quick to make a decision to throw it out and go shopping for a new one. What a waste. Not to mention the cost.

How about doing something different? With some time and effort there are many things that we can fix up to look as good as new (or even better) Fixing things will not only save you money but give you a real sense of satisfaction. You could even take it one step further and make something. Be creative, use your imagination to build or make something. Have a go at 'upcycling' where you take something like an old piece of furniture that is a bit tatty and give it a new lease of life. It might just need repainting or could just require some new material to brighten it up.

The other great result of deciding to fix something is the reduced environment impact because you are throwing away less. You only have to visit your local recycling centre to see the tonnes of 'rubbish' people throw away. It is great that so much now gets recycled but a lot does still go to landfill.

Sewing could be a new skill for you to learn. It really is simple enough for almost everyone. Have a go at mending that jacket, blanket or reattaching that button to your old trousers.

For those of you with children in some form of Scouting, or the Girl Guide movement, sewing will come in very handy when your children start being awarded merit badges for the work they do.

Do you know how to change the wheel on your car? This is another quick fix. Being able to change your wheel is an essential skill that can really get you out of a sticky situation. Imagine being on your way to an important appointment. Would you have time to wait 1-2 hours for a recovery vehicle to come out and change your wheel? Rather than wait, you could be up and running again in less that fifteen minutes. Go and have a practice today!

There is another way to look at 'Fix'. Maybe there is a relationship or friendship in your life that is, let's call it 'broken'. By 'broken' we mean that you have not spoken with this other person for some time. Ask yourself, why did it happen in the first place? How has it got to this?

When you think about that broken relationship or friendship how does it make you feel? Does it by any chance sadden you, because once they might have been your best friend? You could hold out an olive branch to this person by making a call or sending a short text message asking how they are. We are not saying it will be easy or that everything will be fixed overnight but it will be one step closer. We waste so much energy mulling over imaginary conversations in our heads, or tell ourselves unhelpful thoughts like, 'they won't want to talk to me' or 'what is the point?' Well there is a point!

You can either fix broken relationships or get closure. Either way, it's a darn site better than festering on it.

Image you hear a rattling noise on your car. Do you get it fixed or wait until it breaks down because an important part has fallen off? By that stage it is too late, the damage has been done. If you feel that a relationship you have is not in the best shape, do something now to fix it becomes too big.

Hmm! Moment:
Over the next 7 days think about a relationship you have with a particular person which is not where you would like it to be. Think about how you could reach out to this person in an attempt to rebuild a friendship you once had. Then, and this is the important part, act now. Do something, send a text, make a call or send an email. Do something rather than nothing. Your friendships have so much more value than you know.

27. Ear

People often ask, 'When coaching someone, how much should I talk and how much should be saying?' my answer, 'You have one mouth and two ears, use them in that proportion.' Might sound simple enough, but some people love the sound of their own voice. You know the ones I'm talking about, the ones who just seem to go on and on, and on. You can probably hear their voice right now, you know who I mean, don't you?

In Chapter 15 'See' we first mentioned that the vast majority of the world's population have five sensory preferences in which to take in information. From studies carried out 'sight' accounts for the largest percentage, closely followed by 'Auditory.' so let's delve into this preference more.

In Dr. Stephen Covey's very successful book 'The 7 Habits of Highly Effective People' he talked and described the 5th habit as 'Seek first to understand, then to be understood' this essentially means we first need to listen to the other person before opening your mouth and putting your point of view across. When we say listen, we are not talking on a superficial level otherwise known, as 'nodding dog' but truly listening to what the other person has to say. Turning down the volume inside your own head of the questions you feel the need to ask, but instead listen to them empathically to truly understand.

Covey, Stephen R. *The 7 Habits of Highly Effective People*. Simon and Schuster. 2004 (reprinted edition)

Open your ears and your heart so you not only hear the words being spoken but you connect with the feelings and sentiment that's attached to them.

Too really listen remove any and if possible all distractions that can affect your ability to truly listen. Put your mobile phone on silent and away in a pocket or bag, shut off your PC screen or close your laptop for a few moments. What about finding a different location away from other people who might disturb you. Imagine for a second that the person you are listening to is telling you information that will save your life… will that get your focus? Maybe they are telling you how to win the lottery? Whatever thought you need, think it for a moment so that your brain is engaged and focussing on only one task…. listening.

Hmm moment:

Take yourself outside, you might want to go into your garden or go to a local park. Sit down comfortably, take in several deep breaths and relax, remember 'air' is good. Now either close your eyes, or cast your gaze down and listen to the sounds around you. Really listen; what sounds do you hear? You might feel the urge to look up to see where the noise is coming from, resist. Pay just the noises you hearing around you, your full attention.

What do you hear? Listen out for the sounds of nature, birds chirping or leaves rustling in the gentle breeze. If thoughts appear in your mind, notice them and then allow them to float away again.

Try moving your focus from all the noises to just one, listen for the birdsong, then to the wind in the trees, to the dog barking in the distance. Notice how much more you are aware of, when you really focus your listening.

28. Hot

Who doesn't like a little bit of spice in their lives? It's great on occasions to hot things up. We mentioned it earlier, getting outside and feeling the sun on your face is lovely, not only for your spirits but it also good for your body. Sunlight releases Vitamin 'D' which you need. Getting away on a holiday to somewhere hot can really lift your mood. You may have been planning sometime in the sun for months and before you know it you are actually lying on the beach with your favourite book, with people you love spending time with. How about having a hot sauna or going into a steam room again these are fantastic for your body as well as it helps cleanse and invigorate the body.

So being 'hot' can be good but what about when we get hot under the collar?

When we mentioned that exciting holiday, the relaxing sauna or the refreshing walk in the sun do you expect it to be 'perfect'? That is an interesting expectation. Have you ever noticed how much people talk about the weather, more often than not they are generally complaining about it? Why is that? In our experience it's because of their expectation. In July we generally expect it to be hot and sunny so we complain when it rains but we are less likely to complain in April because that's when we expect showers.

In our lives many people have unrealistic expectations. Now before we get into this we are not saying "life's all doom and gloom and not worth living" (because much of it is fantastic!) but we are saying that you should have realistic expectations about the world and people or there is a good chance that you are going to be feeling upset or let down quite a lot.

The next time you drive anywhere do you expect all the roads to be clear? Do you expect all other drivers to be courteous and professional? If so, get ready for disappointment. A more real expectation here is that roads are busy and there is a chance that every so often you will get stuck in traffic and let's face it whilst most drivers will be safe, some will make the occasional mistake or simply make bad choices when driving. That's life!

Hmm moment:
Write out a list of the top 5 things that generally annoy, frustrate or upset you. For each one write out a few expectations that you have of the situation, other people or maybe even yourself. Now challenge each of those and write down a more realistic expectation. Setting these down in writing and actively challenging unrealistic expectations will help give you a more positive mindset for the future and you'll feel more equipped to deal with life's challenges.

29. Hug

A hug, really? Yes, really. Think about it for a moment, we are social beings who need to connect with others, not just mentally and emotionally but physically too. Remember in Chapter 25, we spoke about having a 'Pet,' stroking or hugging a cat or dog can and does relieve stress.

In this chapter we are going to focus our attention on the third aspect, physical. What do they do to punish prisoners? They place them in solitary confinement on occasions for prolonged periods of time depending on the severity of the crime. Because keeping an individual in isolation away from others, unable to talk to or interact in any way with other can be soul destroying.

Let us take you back to a time when you were younger. Can you remember what you used to do when you came out of school and your Mum or Dad was standing at the gates waiting for you? You more than lightly, when you saw them standing there, ran as fast as you could and gave them a big hug and it was incredibly satisfying.

Hugs are funny things and we feel that they come in three forms:

1. A greeting, more often than not this is initiated with a handshake, but then the 2 individuals step into one another and possibly put their arm or arms around the other

person's back, before patting them on the back. If it is a more formal situation and the other person wasn't expecting it, this might be a bit awkward depending on how well they know one another.

2. An expression of love or affection, this is more like the Mum & Dad situation above, this is the hug where two people press themselves against each other, often putting both arms around one another and giving them a squeeze, we will call this a 'proper hug.' This is the type of hug you give someone when you want to give them when you are so pleased to see them or without the use of words say "it'll be ok" or "I'm here for you" You know the hug we mean.

3. Appreciation, this one probably sits somewhere between the other 2. This is the type of hug someone will give you when they really appreciate what you have done for them. A time when you have made a difference to them in some way, you might have given them something of a material nature or knowledge.

This is the sciencey bit; research shows that giving or receiving a proper, meaningful hug is the quickest way for you to get what is known as oxytocin flowing around your body.

http://news.bbc.co.uk/1/hi/4131508.stm

What is an oxytocin? It is also known as the 'love drug,' therefore is helps give your emotions a boost which in turn will calm you down. How does it do this? Oxytocin when released into our bodies:

- Lowers the cortisol levels (another natural chemical in your body), enabling us to achieve a better quality of sleep and
- Lowers blood pressure.

Hmm moment:

When was the last time you gave someone a hug? I mean a proper hug to let them know you appreciate what they have done for you or as a sign of love and affection? Hugs make us healthier, happier and more connected with other so what is not to love about giving them?

Over the next 7 days think of three people who mean something to you and give them a good, proper hug.

30. Toy

One question that never fails to get an interesting reaction when working with groups is "What was your favourite or most memorable toy as a child?" This can also be followed up by "and how does that show up in your life now?" Recalling favourite toys sparks joyful memories and will usually bring a smile to anyone's face.

Try it now; take a few moments to recall it. Maybe it was Lego, a doll, a bike or a game like hungry hippos! Or for the younger generation maybe even an Xbox or PlayStation. Those who loved Lego may even find they entered a career that fulfils on a larger scale the ability to build or create things. The bike lover might love travelling, enjoying the sense of adventure and the ability to get out and exercise. We are not going to go into a whole load of child psychology, that is not our expertise but please take these concepts into the here and now. What can you do with this knowledge?

In the 1990's movie Peter's Friends, there is a quote that has stuck with me 'Adults are children with money.' We may not have toys per say as adults but 'play' really does have massive benefits for all of us. In a fantastic book by Dr. Stuart Brown, 'Play: How It Shapes the Brain, Opens the Imagination, and Invigorates the Soul,' he emphasises how much we learn and develop by playing.

Peters Friends. Written by Rita Rudner and Martin Bergman. Directed and produced by Kenneth Branagh. 1992
Brown, Dr. Stuart. Play: How It Shapes the Brain, Opens the Imagination, and Invigorates the Soul. J P Tarcher/Penguin Putnam 2010 (reprinted edition)

So how do we 'play' at home or at work and not have people think we are being childish in a negative way. Think of a recent team building event you have attended, you are in essence playing with the view and aim of developing understanding and it is far more fun and engaging than just sitting listening to someone talk you through a concept.

As well as the benefits for us of playing, what happens when we give time to play with our own children? Taking time out to play creates a bond as seen in the animal kingdom many times over. And animals don't need to be told to do this! Understanding and being part of your child's fun and imagination really does strengthen the relationship and creates fantastic memories for those involved.

Back in 2006 Sir Ken Robinson author and educationist gave a TED talk, entitled 'Do schools kill creativity?' In fact, it's one of the top 10 most watched TED talks. In this talk he described how schools teach individuals to conform rather than embrace differences. We go much more with the thought process Ken spoke about, there are a number of different intelligences but schools focus more on the literacy and numeracy. Steve Jobs had the right idea; he was once quoted as saying, '...embrace the crazy ones...' When you have a problem, go more childlike in your thinking. Stop over-complicating what is going on.

https://www.ted.com/talks/ken_robinson_says_schools_kill_creativity

Let's take a look at a real-life example:

It is Christmas Eve and Santa has just delivered all the children's presents. On this occasion however a very young girl lives in this house, along with an older brother, their Mummy and Daddy. Upon realising it is Christmas morning the girl and everyone else in the house run down the stairs to see what awaits them. The little girl has received a massive box which contains the Barbie castle she desired from the moment she saw it in the shop and the parents look at one another knowingly, rather pleased with themselves (for some reason). The ever loving parents soon get stuck in to help their little girl take the castle from the box and immediately started playing with.

This is then the kicker! Within a relatively short period of time she bores of the nice new pink Barbie castle and begins playing with the empty box. Much to the parent's bewilderment. For the little girl the box is no longer a box, it is anything she wants it to be and more because she uses her imagination, her mind is free to see potential. That is what we want to get across here; having toys and playing more with things can help you to free your mind and it can take you back to a time where anything and everything is possible.

Hmm moment:
Take some time and think about the more mundane tasks you complete day in, day out. What can you do to make them more interesting? How can you make work into 'play'? If you have children, ask them what they would do to make things more fun. We truly believe working for Lego would be the best job, ever. We would even go as far as to say it would be AWESOME!!!

31. Out

How much of your time do you spend indoors compared to outdoors? Too often people get up in the morning get ready, hop straight into their car and whilst driving keep all their doors and windows closed, then once in the car park walk straight inside to start work. They don't venture out at lunchtime and then repeat that process in reverse in the evening followed by a night staring aimlessly at the TV, mobile phone, tablet or computer screen.

There are a number big issues right there! Are you one of those people who follows a habit? Some of which we have covered in other chapters such as 'Air' and 'Yes.' Fresh air is so much better for you than air-conditioning and in 'Gym,' we discussed how lack of movement or exercise in your day and how it can affect us. But here now we'd like you to think about what else you might find when you step outside, not just physically but outside of your current routines or habits that are continually getting you the same results.

Let us take a look at the physical 'out' to begin with. It is a wonderful feeling to get back to nature. The next time you get a chance, get out of the office building you spend nearly a third of your day in and go for a short walk round the block taking time to notice things you have maybe whizzed past in your car on a daily basis and not really paid much attention to. So often you will see signs, buildings, people and more that you never even knew existed.

If you are at home, then whenever possible get out into the garden. Going back to nature helps you get back to the simple things in life. These simple things remind us that we don't actually need a lot of the purchases we surround ourselves with and we certainly don't need all the stress we put ourselves under, buying things to impress people we may not know or even like that much.

Whilst outside you might even bump into a neighbour or colleague and have an interesting conversation, strike up a friendship or even find a future partner! If you have children, then consider taking them to a farm go see and feed some animals like a pig or cow. You might even want to go to an owl sanctuary to watch these fascinating creatures. Whatever you do, get back to nature, enjoy it and be in the present moment rather than letting your thoughts race away from you. People who enjoy their lives live much longer than those who don't!

Now what about mentally getting 'out'. Often we get stuck in a rut or simply follow the same routines we have always followed because we don't know what else there is to try or we simply haven't even considered it. You may have heard of the comfort, stretch and panic zones. We spend much of our lives in the comfort zone because after all, it's comfortable there. There is a drawback to that, we easily become stale, bored or tired and we are definitely not learning anything new here. Have you thought about how important it is to keep learning?

The world, technology, work, people and just about anything we can think of to write here is changing at a more dramatic rate than ever before so our ability to learn is key to us being successful in the modern world.

For many, school was not a great learning experience due to pressure to achieve, starting to understand ourselves and the world around us and peer pressure to be liked and to fit in rather than be different. Ask anyone who learned to drive. Ok, not every lesson would have been great but each time we learn a new manoeuvre we feel that buzz excitement and pride. We have learned something new that we had not previously known how to do and we put it into practice. If you haven't learnt how to drive think about learning how to swim or ride a bicycle. When we learn that our best friend is pregnant or engaged to be married we feel joy. Learning doesn't have to mean reading from books!

Act moment:

Today (or tomorrow if you're reading this late at night) go somewhere you have never been before. This could maybe be into a shop you have never been into or maybe a walk round a nearby park at lunchtime. Appreciate all the benefits these bring you. Start doing this at least once a week and you will soon feel like an explorer, boldly going to new places you have never been to before. As you get used to this you will start becoming more adventurous, walking further and seeing so much more of what life has to offer.

32. Ace

Each of us in life gets dealt a different hand. Some have rich parents, the majority however do not, and our parents give us as many opportunities as they can with the resources available to them. Some have a great education, others do not. Some are born healthy, others are not. We do not know which you fall into, so maybe the cards are not stacked in your favour. How do you know if you have been dealt an Ace card or not? And how does this affect you?

It is very easy to see the evidence that backs up our beliefs about ourselves, other people and the world in general. We are sure you could easily list some well educated people who are now politicians, business people or entrepreneurs. You could also list people you know who grew up in poverty, failed at school (or maybe school failed them) who now are making nothing or very little of their lives. Now you can be understood for thinking, yes, cause and effect, good things cause good results, poor things cause poor results. But if this is your thinking you are only looking at it from one perspective, your perspective. If you really looked around you, you would also find people who seemed to be dealt an 'ace' card, great life etc. who are now struggling whether mentally, financially or in their relationships. You could also find people who were dealt a 'two' who are now successful, happy and thriving, enjoying life's challenges and considering themselves a real success.

So what about you? Do you feel life has dealt you an ace card? Or the two of spades? How might your view about what is and isn't possible of someone from your background be limiting your ability to improve your own life? Take a pen and paper and write a few sentences starting "People like me can…" & "People like me can't…" and then to finish write a few answers to "People like me have the opportunity to…" Aim to write 3-5 answers minimum to each one.

Here are a few of our own examples that might help get you thinking:

People like me can…. Always learn more.
People like me can't…. Become CEO's.
People like me have the opportunity to travel the world

How did you get on? This can be a great opportunity to really do some soul searching and learning about your own personal 'truth'. We say truth because usually what we believe becomes the truth. If we dare to dream and act a little bigger, then we create a new truth.

So getting an 'ace' card is all about you, not about others. In tennis an 'ace' is where you score a point by serving the ball past your opponent without them touching it. You win, they lose. What we are saying here is that being dealt an 'ace' card is about you, nobody else.

It's not about trying to be better than anyone else, it's about being the best you can be. There will always be someone wealthier than you (the only exception is one person in the world!). There will always be someone fitter than you. There will always be someone who seems to have a better life in some way or shape. But it's not about them. It is about you getting the right combination of being happy with what you have and constantly striving to improve the lives of not only yourself but the lives of others around you.

A great question to ask yourself is "Am I a little better than I was yesterday?" Maybe you have learned something new or you've got to know a friend a little better. Maybe you stopped to help a stranger by giving them directions or helping them change a flat tire. Maybe you have done one of the many other things we recommend in this book. If you can answer "yes" to this question, then we salute you. In our opinion YOU ARE ACE!

Hmm moment:

Every morning when you wake up, say to yourself "I'm ACE because...." and to get the most from this come up with a new answer every day. This is an amazing activity to really help you have a more positive attitude and we know that more good comes to those with a positive outlook.

33. Got

More often than not we focus on what we haven't got, instead of telling ourselves what we have got. In fact, we more often than not compare ourselves to people we don't even know or on occasions don't even like and look at what they've got. This is wrong, so wrong. Instead ask yourself, 'what resources have I got that can help you?'

We believe you should be more thankful for and focused on the things we have got in our lives. If you are reading this, then you have got your sight, a truly marvellous gift, according to the World Health Organisation (WHO) there is an estimated 285 million people who are visually impaired worldwide: 39 million are blind. Therefore, you have the ability to see a sun rising and children playing in the snow during the winter.

Maybe you are listening to this as an audible book, according to the World Federation for the Deaf, there are approximately 70 million deaf people who use sign language as their first language or mother tongue, they do not have the opportunity to listen to birds singing in the morning, or an orchestra playing Mozart or Handel.

World Health Organisation article: http://www.who.int/mediacentre/factsheets/fs282/en/

When you think about your friends and family, do you ever stop to truly appreciate what you have got? Think about the people in your life who you love and who love you. The people who care for you, support you, help you no matter what the situation is. You really have got something special. Maybe people rely on you for these things so another thing you have 'got' is responsibility. Do you take personal responsibility for your actions?

Think about your health, often we neglect to think about this because of the busy world we believe we live in. We often don't appreciate what we have got until we lose it and by then it is too late. How often do you wake up and say "great, I feel normal today!" I'm sure it is very seldom, if at all, but we do notice when we have a cold, a sprain or an injury or even worse, 'Man Flu!' The challenge we men have with this is that no woman really understands how debilitating this can be for us mere mortal men.

Have you considered what opportunities you have? We live in a mobile world and as transportation continues to improve, global mobility will get even easier, the fact is you have got the opportunity to live and work anywhere in the world. You can trade with anyone on almost any continent by using the internet. You can share your message with the world on YouTube or other social media sites. You have got massive opportunity for personal development - not just by reading this book, but by putting it into action.

Hmm moment:

How do you use your daily commute to work? Do you listen to music or personal development books? Think about how you can make better use of your time. Remember we discussed in Chapter 12 - 'Day' that each and every one of us have 86400 seconds a day to use and we cannot carry this time forward, but you can invest it in developing yourself. What other resources have you got that you could use more?

34. Say

Do you always have your say? Do you speak about what is on your mind? If you answered yes to both questions, fantastic, why not just skip this chapter and move on? Or you could tell that voice in your head to pipe down for a moment and see what more you can learn.

We're sure you've heard of Mountaineer and philanthropist Edmund Hillary, the first person to conquer Mount Everest. He once said 'People do not decide to become extraordinary. They decide to accomplish extraordinary things' and we truly believe there is a big difference between what is going on in our heads compared to what we externalise, and act upon.

You, me, everybody has a unique voice so it really is up to us to use it. There is a particular phrase that we keep being drawn back to time and again and it's this: Would you prefer to be a voice or an echo? Nobody else on this planet has had the exact same experiences as you, therefore you have a different perspective to others and you should be heard. You will have different ideas, great! Irrespective of what someone's position or seniority is in a business, it doesn't always make them right. We are all equal and every voice counts as just as much as the next.

https://en.wikiquote.org/wiki/Edmund_Hillary

The other challenge we encounter more often than not on a daily basis is that some people say a lot and we mean A LOT! Do you know the people we mean, you hear a lot of words, but you get nothing? Plato is quoted as saying "Wise men speak because they have something to say; Fools because they have to say something." Oh how true this unfortunately is.

Social media is playing a greater part in our everyday lives and probably will in years to come, so the question to ask yourself is 'are you the person who reposts everyone else's thoughts?' or do you generate new content to help others think differently? Stop being a sheep, following the rest of the flock. Break free and stand out by saying and doing something different

Hmm moment:

Take a moment, ask yourself 'What difference am I going to make to the world today?' Notice the difference between thinking and saying. Now take the time to think about other conversations you have had or will be having over the next few days or weeks, those things that you may have been putting off and say out loud, 'What do I want to achieve from this conversation?' then act upon it. Do not bottle it up, take the opportunities. Carpe Diem, seize the day!

35. Not

As well as knowing who you want to be and what you want to do it is also important to know what you do not want from life. Maybe you want to be a senior manager but you do not want to miss out on your children growing up. You might want to run your own business but do not want to work weekends. You might want to spend lots of time with your partner but do not want to lose the relationship you have with your friends. This may seem like a difficult balance but the reality is many of us currently balance these kind of things even though we are not consciously aware of it and we're not making conscious choices.

Consider some of your aims from chapter 2. These are important to you but what are you not prepared to do while achieving them? Your aim may have been to get fit but you are not prepared to spend every evening at the gym. How about finding a 3 day a week programme? You could get up and out earlier, go to the gym before work and still have your evenings free. Now you have more, not less choices. Find your own example now and give it a go.

Your 'not' might not be a physical thing, it could be one of your personal values that you're not prepared to compromise. You might want to have a new career but you're not prepared to work for an unethical company. We looked at values in Chapter 11 so go back and review them if you need to.

From another angle we need to consider how we use the word 'not' in an unhelpful way. Many people when faced with a new challenge say "I'm not like that." It could be anything from being confident to being good at public speaking or it could be being creative or organised. Rather than immediately dismissing the challenge you should try saying "I need to learn how to become like that to fulfil my dreams". This is one of the best mindset shifts that you can have.

Consider the potential opportunities in life you could have (or already have) missed out on because you simply thought "I'm not like that" or "I'm not that kind of person". Much of this has come from your upbringing and is often completely unconscious to us. Ask a group of children "who wants to draw a picture?" and they will all put their hands up. Ask the same question to adults and you will get a very different result! Many will without thinking quickly reply "I'm not creative" or "I can't draw" or "It's just not me! Rather than more narrowly defining ourselves as we grow older we should aim to widen our skills, abilities and interests.

Take a minute now to consider what you think you are not. Here's a few examples: Adventurous, fun, an entrepreneur, clever, optimistic, a high achiever, confident, a potential millionaire, relationship material, and a success. Hopefully that list has not depressed you and you are still reading.

So what is the answer? Well simply when you catch yourself saying "I'm not like that" then immediately say "I need to learn to be like that". This quick shift tells yourself that learning is important and it is something that you can do. Then you start learning; reading books, magazines and articles, watching people who are good at what you want to be good at, talking to them and finding out how they think, what they do and how they behave.

Hmm moment:
Lastly we have one more top tip to help you with that word 'not'. Have you ever said the phrase "I'm not sure?" We all have at times. The simple reply to that statement which you can say to yourself or others is "If you were sure, what would you think/do". This fantastic question allows the brain to consider the possibility of being sure and accessing more of its amazing capacity. Give it a try the next time you are not sure about something.

36. Tip

For thousands of years, man has learned from stories passed down through the generations. Many of these stories are aimed to teach a lesson or share some wisdom or morals. The intention is always to help the recipient in some way. In this chapter we will look at the advice you receive and allow you to choose if it is right for you. Not all advice is good!

People will often give you some form of advice or tips to get on in life. Consider for a moment; what is the best tip someone who is important to you has given you? Maybe it came from a complete stranger. It could have had a really big impact on you. As with any advice, some you will take in and use and in time it becomes an important part of your life. In other instances, you will dismiss it, never to be thought about again.

You probably have some 'family wisdom' that has been passed on from generation to generation which family members have lived by it without really understanding or questioning where it came from. Have you ever stopped to check that it is really benefitting you in your life, today? Yes, it may have been good advice for the past but the world has moved on. It may have been good advice for others but that does not mean it will be good for you; we all have different needs and walk different paths.

The tip that the person is giving you may be based on their own limiting beliefs and insecurities or on their shortcomings which they may be unwittingly projecting onto you. "Never talk to strangers" might be good advice for a child but as you grow up you need to talk to people you have never met before or you will soon find you have very few friends. People who have had certain experiences might think they are helping when they tell you to "not take too many risks" but their good intentions could be holding you back from the adventure of a lifetime. Take tips from others but check they work for you.

The other place in our lives where we regularly use the word 'tip' is in a restaurant or café, or maybe for your hairdresser or a taxi driver. Why do you leave a tip? Is it because you feel you need to, because that is 'what you do', or is it because the person has gone above and beyond what you expected and you want to show you really appreciate what they have done?

Giving a tip in a restaurant is seen differently by people and we get that. What we say though is, if someone has done their job but surprised and delighted you in how they went about it, then dig a little deeper and reward that. You may be in a much more financially secure place, so pay it forward and put a smile on their faces and make their day.

Hmm Moment:

Take some time and really think about this: What is the top tip you can give someone to challenge their way of thinking to support their personal or professional growth?

The next time you are in a restaurant rather than just looking at server, look around you and see what they are contending with. If they are 'run off their feet' and still take the time to deliver great service, then acknowledge that either internally or externally and show your appreciation of what they are dealing with at that time. Not just money, give them your verbal thanks too.

37. New

New can be something recently made, discovered, created or purchased. It could be an antique but it could be new to you. We celebrate the New Year and a new baby boy or girl. Getting a new job can be an exciting new chapter in our lives. So, out with the old in with the new?

Yes, we love getting something new. It's wonderful being able to go out and purchase that new thing you wanted, irrespective of whether it is a new car costing £30,000 or a new pair of shoes at £30 or maybe even £300 if that's your thing. So value and go for the new but sometimes new can mean change which many people struggle with, old can be comforting and easy. The choice is yours.

When was the last time you received something new, maybe it was a Birthday or Christmas present? What a great feeling carefully opening the present in anticipation of what it might be. New things have a look and a feel about them that is hard to beat. On occasions there may be even a smell, that's right a smell. What is it like getting into a new car? The fresh smell of leather, or untouched plastic or veneer or a newly released book the one you've been waiting weeks to get your hands on, marvellous isn't it?

Let's now bring this even closer to home, even closer to you. What do you think and how does it make you feel when you get dressed in new clothes or shoes for the first time? We often feel better about ourselves and that's great because when you look good, you often feel good. It may be momentary or you may receive compliments throughout the day from others, when they notice the small changes you've made. The thing to remember is you made the choice to make a change to do something new and by doing this you are in control. So, what do you want the new you to look and feel like?

Do not get us wrong, it is not all about spending money. Sometimes it can much simpler, it might be having new experiences, as the saying goes variety is the spice of life. Mixing things up and doing something new or different helps break habitual routines we often fall into. What new experiences do you want to have in your life? Could it be travelling to a new country you've never been to, or driving along in an open top car or maybe you should eat a new flavour of ice-cream. Hopefully by this point in the book you've made positive changes in your life and started to create the new you or discovered you had some talents you never even knew.

Have you recently made any new friends or do you have the same ones since school? Yes, we believe in sticking by great friends but some friends add more value to your life than others. Some of your friends will support the new you and some will hold you back, not wanting you to deviate too far from the you, they have known for years. Finding some new friends can be invigorating giving you new ideas and a fresh outlook. New friends won't cling on to the old you and will take you for who you are now and not who you used to be.

Hmm moment:

Take some time to consider how much you have changed in the last year or the last 5 years. Have you been sailing along the same route or has life thrown challenges at you that made you change? Now think where you would like to be in 1-5 years' time? What will the new you look like? A great way to do this is to write out a list of new things you would like to try. Really challenge yourself here, don't just go for the easy options. Maybe learn a new language, cook a new meal each week or get a whole new wardrobe! Getting involved in something new may also bring along a new set of friends and expand your social network.

38. Sad

The Greek philosopher Aristotle back as early as the 4th century B.C. attempted to identify the exact number of core emotions humans exhibited. He suggested there were 14 which were called the 'irreducible emotions', however in more recent years prominent Psychologist Robert Plutchik, a Professor at the Albert Einstein College of Medicine in his research stated that there are 8 basic emotions: Joy, trust, fear, surprise, sadness, anticipation, anger and disgust. The one we'll focus on here is sadness.

You may be thinking that having a chapter called 'sad' is rather odd in a book all about well-being and personal development so let us explain. If you have never felt sad then how would you know what happy felt like? You may not like feeling sad but life is what it is at times you just can't avoid it. You should accept that all emotions have a purpose.

Understanding and expressing your emotions is an important thing to do for you own mental wellbeing. For the past 20-30 years 'being healthy' has been focused on looking after yourself physically but now more and more is being researched and reported on individual's mental state. It is something that we weren't prepared to talk about openly and many people would suffer in silence or feel stupid admitting they had mental health problems.

https://en.wikipedia.org/wiki/Contrasting_and_categorization_of_emotions#Plutchik.27s_wheel_of_emotions

All that is changing now. Remember if your head is not in a good place, it will show. Trust us on this one. Sigmund Freud said 'we leak the truth.' And we do whether we realise it or not.

To improve your mental health firstly you need to be aware of it. Internally, do you notice how you are feeling day to day, hour by hour? If someone was to ask you to describe your specific emotions, could you? Are you happy, excited or even ecstatic? Take a few moments now to notice the intensity of each of those words for you. How does your body react when you say each word? Life feels so much more vibrant when we can truly explain how we feel. It is perfectly alright and if anything we'd encourage it even more to let people know if you are feeling sad.

Once you are aware that you feel sad then you can consider what it was that caused the emotion. What are you allowing into your life? It could be watching the news, reading a story or something that has happened to you or a loved one. It could be you are dwelling on something from the past that you no longer want to be having that impact on you. People say that time is a healer but just how much time? Is now a good time to move on? As you become more aware of your emotions and where they come from you can start to make better choices.

Recognising emotions in others is key too. Can you tell when your best friend is just a little upset, sad, down, depressed or suicidal? Understanding the level of emotion will allow you to be there to support them as and when needed.

The next time you are with your friends, get off your own agenda and focus on them. Pause and take a really good look at them. Try to guess exactly what emotions they are feeling when they are telling you stories of their recent adventures. Believe us, they will really appreciate your undivided attention.

Hmm Moment:

As with any other part of this book we do not aim to give you medical advice nor is what we offer comparable to the professional help you can get when you need it. What we hope is through making simple choices and changes to your life you will never get to the stage where you need professional help. Unfortunately, we can't control what happens in your life we can only offer you every success with challenges you face.

Write out a list of things that make you sad on the left hand side of a piece of paper. On the right now make a list of things that make you glad. Now compare the two lists. Do you need to remove some from the left? Maybe you need to add some more to the right? Decide now what you will do to lessen your negative emotions and increase the positive.

39. Cut

By this point in the book you may be thinking 'This stuff is all well and good but how am I supposed to fit it all into an already busy life'. And you would be right to think that. It is very easy to take on more and more whether at work because your boss demands it or at home because your family demands it and then find that it all becomes too much.

So let us cut to the chase. You need to cut stuff out as well as adding. Yes, we are talking about removing something, or maybe just reducing it, cutting down. It could be permanently or it could be temporary. So, what thing or things could you cut from your life that are not benefiting you? Could you take a metaphorical axe and chop whatever it is out of your life?

Ask yourself are you prepared to cut things or people from your life that are not helping? Maybe you could just cut down the amount of time you spend with that really negative person. Have you let someone in your life play such a role that you are unable to cut the apron strings? Cut the ties with a harmful or hurtful thing that is taking you on a downward spiral. If you need to, move to a different city or country for a clean cut. Ok, maybe that is a bit drastic but you get the idea; you need to do whatever works.

Another action you can take is have a 'spring clean' by cutting lots of unwanted clothes from your wardrobe. We recommend that you give them to a charity shop rather than throwing them away as giving back to society is great and reduces waste. The general rule to follow here is if you have not worn it for 6 months then get rid! The only exceptions are specific winter and summer clothes. Anything else goes. By getting rid of the old you are making space for something new, potentially something even more exciting or simply reducing down the already difficult choice. Gok Wan (English fashion consultant, author and TV Personality) recommends 18 key items for women and 13 for men which we are sure is a lot less than most people have. President Barack Obama said he had just 2 different coloured suits to reduce the unnecessary choice. So go reduce your wardrobe now.

Something else we would definitely endorse is to cut down on your internet usage. A report in The National Student in July 2016 stated "too much time on the internet could damage your immune system". An Ofcom report in August 2016 stated "more than 60% of teenagers admitted neglecting school work because of surfing the net" and "47% of people blamed internet use as a main reason for not getting enough sleep". We recommend a digital detox. Try small to start with.

http://www.thenationalstudent.com/National/2016-07-09/spending_too_much_time_on_the_internet_could_damage_your_immune_system.html

https://www.ofcom.org.uk/about-ofcom/latest/media/media-releases/2016/cmr-uk-2016

Maybe go for a 30 to 60-minute walk without your phone. Ideally go away on holiday and lock your phone in the safe all week. Take a digital camera too so that you are not tempted to get your phone out.

If you feel like your boss expects you to be responding to calls, texts and emails at all hours of the day and night then we would challenge whether this as an 'effective working style' or simply an overly-stressed boss who struggles to switch off themselves. Try to avoid getting drawn into following their behaviours. Agree what works for you and what doesn't. Cut down on work when you should be benefitting from switching off.

Hmm Moment:
What can you cut out of your life to make way for something new? This may be something physical or habits have you got yourself into to that are not helping you become the person you want to be. Think of one thing you can reduce or cut out completely and aim to achieve it within a reasonable timescale.

40. One

As we mentioned in our introduction to this book, life can be complicated, in fact really complicated on occasions and often we tell ourselves we will do this and that but before you know it, you have a list as long as your arm of things you say you will do and you probably never actually get round to completing any of them because the list appears insurmountable.

Our suggestion, keep it simple, really simple and only do one thing at a time. That's achievable right? 'How do you eat an elephant? One chunk at a time.' The point we are making here is to at least start doing something, rather than nothing. Often you find that by completing one task, then another you start to gain momentum and the desire to keep going. With this momentum you also get a sense of achievement which can be, and is very satisfying.

Ask yourself these questions:

What one thing can I action today to move me closer to my aim?
What's the one thing missing in my life right now?
What's that one thing I've been putting off and should act upon now?
If today was my last day, what one thing would I love to do?

A great technique we're sure you will agree to get you going, for overcoming that dreaded procrastination is to aim to complete just one thing. Yes, that's right, one thing at a time. People are often of the preconception that they can multitask and complete many tasks at once, you might be able to do what appears to be several things at a time, the truth and research has shown this is that it's just not true. You can only truly focus on one thing at a time.

You may have already tried this with a small child when attempting to feed them; 'Just try one spoonful,' which hopefully leads to the 2nd, then a 3rd and so on and so on right up to the point they have finished eating the entire bowl of food.

Maybe you want to get fit and decide to do 20 push-ups a day. For some, the thought of doing 20 would be likened to conquering Everest and we are sure it's not. All you need to commit to is to do 1 push-up a day. In your mind you might think "only one, easy!" because it sounds so much more manageable and easier to get started. The idea here is that once you have done your 1 push-up you are much more likely to think 'while I'm here I may as well do 10'.

What a great way to get you started and if you do only just do the one, maybe each day this week you do one more, every day. You will soon get into the swing of it.

Hmm moment:

There are two things to for you to think about and before you say it, we know we have been talking about doing just one thing. It's alright we are the authors we can do that.

Firstly, take a moment and reflect on what is your one biggest achievement to date in my life? Why did you choose that particular event? What made it so special?

Secondly rather than putting that thing off any longer, you know the thing we are talking about, act on it right NOW, what is your number one priority today? What is that one thing you can do today to move you towards your aim? Sit down and think about what that one thing is and act!

41. Win

What does it mean to be a winner? How often do you get to win? In fact, how often do you consider yourself a winner?

Okay let's get started. When did you last win? And we don't mean the lottery! To 'win' can be considered from the old or middle English where it meant "joy, rapture, pleasure, delight, gladness". All very positive feelings, right? Or it can relate to 'to labour, toil, trouble oneself; resist, oppose, contradict; fight, strive, struggle, rage; endure.'

These might not sound as positive but it is useful to consider that winning isn't always the achievement of gains or massive leaps forwards, sometime it can be surviving and getting through life's challenges. Take a moment now to reconsider your previous answer. When did you last win? And more importantly, what beliefs, thoughts and actions were essential to helping you win?

A great way to ensure you win more often is to take on more challenges. Isn't a challenge far more interesting and motivating than a task or goal. Humans love to be challenged! You only have to take a brief look through history to see the amazing challenges that have been undertaken but people, people like you! Have you ever read the Guinness Book of World Records? There are some really interesting accomplishments in there.

Do you set yourself challenges that get the best out of you? Are you too afraid of losing, therefore you only take on challenges where you know you have a fair to good chance of being able to achieve it? This really will not stretch you enough, our suggestion is to take on more challenges and you will achieve them more often.

Are you one of life's winners? Let's take a look at your attitude towards winning. Do you believe that 'winners are grinners'? Or are you more of the mindset that 'it's not the winning that counts, it's the taking part'? Well our perspective is that if you don't ever aim to win then it is highly unlikely you never will.

Maybe you have a fear of losing? Life's biggest winners are often also life's biggest losers. Peter Jones is an example of a highly successful businessman now but several of his businesses failed when he was younger. Similarly, no athlete, sportsperson or sports team has ever always won. They take part in every race or competition knowing that they might lose but always aim to win. Think about the Olympics, every athlete goes there with the determination and focus with one aim, winning the gold medal.

The legend that is Muhammed Ali is a fantastic example. His mindset was amazing and he was resolute because he considered himself the winner long before the fight ever took place. He visualised his wins before he had them, he even went as far as to say which round he was going to win in.

Now compare this to the disastrous England football team campaign in the 2016 Euros where the manager said to camera "we'll try to stay in the competition as long as possible" - hardly a winner's mentality.

Hmm moment:
Who have you got surrounding you right now? Are you surrounding yourself with people who have a winner's mentality? If you are always surrounded by complainers, those who say "life's not fair" or people who don't take on challenges to stretch themselves then it's highly unlikely that you will too.

Think about your 5 closest friends. Are they people that will help, support, challenge and motivate you to win? If not, who else do you know that is a real winner? Maybe you should have a go spending more time with them. If you don't know enough winners then try looking further afield, maybe a person you work with or people who are in your industry. These days it's easier to connect up with people on social media and find out how they do what they do. Make it your challenge to surround yourself with winners.

42. Sex

Yes, we really have put the word 'Sex' in this book for two reasons.

Firstly, this can change your life in oh so many ways, especially if the right precautions are not taken, if you get what we mean? Sex can be such a crude way of describing when two people (who are meant to love each other) are intimate with one another. The thing to remember here is that if those two people are not careful they could end up, after oh let's say around 9 months with 'them' being a three or four (if they have twins). If on the other hand you are in a same sex relationship, then it would be a little more difficult to end up with a little person but if you do want to become parents then there are alternatives.

On a more serious note though, if you are in a relationship with a member of the opposite sex then life gets all serious and adult because you not only have yourself to look after, you have another little person who is more demanding than the most awkward stakeholder or boss you have ever had.

Why? Because these little people have demands, which can be imposed upon you 24/7, whereas a boss only gets you for between 40 - 45 hours a week. Of course you could work even more if you want to climb that corporate ladder.

Bringing up a child is probably the most taxing whilst most rewarding thing you can possibly do. Don't be scared by the challenge but do ensure you challenge yourselves to be the best possible parents you can be.

Secondly, we are going to list a number different occupations and we would like you to consider and mentally picture the person you believe would be performing that job. Right here we go...

- Doctor
- Florist
- Primary school teacher
- Hairdresser
- Pilot
- Nurse
- Engineer
- Baker

Done!

Be honest with yourself, who did you picture for each? Were they male or female? What age might they have been? The point we are wanting to make here is this; do you have a bias between the sexes? Maybe you yourself have you not gone into a particular profession because it was normally associated as a job for a member of the opposite sex? Seriously! We live in the 21st century, let us think equal opportunities.

In Chapter 23 'Who' we discussed that on occasions people from an older generation imprint their bias on us. We say you should push back on other people's uninformed, limiting and out-of-date beliefs and comments and do what YOU want.

Hmm moment:

If you are unhappy with your current job or maybe wish to find a more fulfilling career or just fancy a change for whatever reason, then write a list of the jobs that interest to you. What would you really enjoy?

Maybe even write out a list of all the jobs you might previously have thought of as for 'someone else' whether a member of the opposite sex, someone with a higher level of education or someone older or younger than yourself. Now look through that list and consider what might actually fit your skills and talents.

43. Yet

Ok then, what is on your bucket list? How many experiences or things that you want to do, have you completed? And how many have you not YET ticked off the list?

Yet is a fantastic word to include in a sentence because you are implying that you haven't quite reached the goal you set yourself, it's something you haven't done up until now. We really are hoping by now that we have been challenging you throughout this book, well if you hadn't realised it yet, you do now. Our aim was to challenge you and limiting beliefs that have potentially held you back because of others insecurities or inadequacies, well no more.

In Chapter 2 'Aim' we discussed the importance of understanding and setting out what your goals are, your aim for the next week, the next month, maybe even the next year. What can you do to get it? You may tell yourself "…but I don't know how to do that!' What we are saying is add the word 'yet' to the end of that short sentence. No time like the present to have a go, go on say it again '…but I don't know how to do that yet!' What difference do you notice, does it sound as final? Doubt it… What is your 'that?' name it. Is it to run your own business? Play a new sport? Use even more technology? Rather than saying "I don't know how to…" always add that simple 3-letter word "yet" to the end of the sentence as this will give you the feeling that it WILL and CAN be something that you will do in the future.

It's all a matter of mindset, but whose mindset? Yours of course, but what is mindset? The best way to describe it is that little voice in your head that talks to you, the funny thing about it is that it talks you into things and can then talk you right back out again in the blink of an eye. The key, turn the volume down.

Hmm Moment:

We think you know the drill by now: Stop, sit down or go for a walk and think about those things you want to do, but do not have the skills for, yet. What do you really want to do or achieve? Once you have decided, understand where you are now and where you want to be. Then get to it and make it happen! Have you started yet?

44. Fit

We have already covered health and fitness in previous sections, particularly Chapter 17 'GYM' so why have a section called FIT? Well this isn't about fitness it's about what fits you and what doesn't. Do you remember the classic picture of a school child stood in a hugely oversized uniform with the parent saying "don't worry, you'll soon grow into it"? Ok, that's fine at school age but once we are fully grown adults it's worth considering what fits and what doesn't and we are not just talking clothes. But that's a good place to start…

Have you ever been to a clothes shop, tried on an item and thought 'well it's not quite right but it's such a good bargain I have to get it?' Chances are, that item is either still in your wardrobe with the label still attached or it was worn once or twice and then off to the charity shop a year or two later.

It is very easy to get caught up by 'a bargain' but it's simply a waste of money if you don't wear it longer than the five minutes you had it on in the changing room. Imagine you buy a T-Shirt for £20 and wear it 40 times. Not too bad at 50p a wear. But another 'bargain' T-Shirt is reduced to just £5 ("wow" we hear you say) but you only wear it once before deciding it's not really you. That T-Shirt has now cost you £5, per wear! That's ten times the cost of the original one. Still consider it a bargain?

What else apart from clothes is it important to get the right fit for? Your job? Partner? Home? Any of these are obviously worth considering. Are you happy to accept something that doesn't really fit you? Yes, we all have to compromise and it's not that often that we find anything or anyone that's 'perfect'. In fact, very little in life is actually perfect so it's not really something worth aiming for and anyhow who is to say what perfect is? But a good fit is worth aiming for.

So how do you recognise what fits and what doesn't? You could write a pro's and con's list but if this is about a prospective partner, don't do what Ross from the TV series Friends did and allow the other person to see it.

A great starting point might be to set out what your 'absolute' criteria is. For a home, this might be the number of bedrooms, the size or garden or the commute to work. Next decide what are the 'nice to haves' which may include style, size of rooms, aspect, location etc. Lastly list what you don't really care about. This may seem a bit pointless but by capturing it you might suddenly realise it should be on one of the other lists. Some of these might be trees in the garden, a driveway, light fittings, carpet style etc.

You will see some great examples of this if you look on dating sites where people answer the 'looking for' section, not that either of us have done this.

For some people you really doubt that they will ever meet anyone because they have been so specific about height, hair colour, interests and more, lots more. Ok, we are not saying "say yes to anything" but at least keep your options slightly more open!

Hmm moment:
We have a couple of things we want you to consider. Firstly, do get those 'bargains' out of your wardrobe and do some good with them, give them to a local charity or homeless shelter it could mean the matter of life or death to someone in a less fortunate position than yourself.

Secondly, think about something in your life that you have not been entirely happy with and have been putting off, draw 2 lines down the page to create 3 columns. At the top of the first column, write 'absolutely must have' at the top of the second, 'nice to have' and the third 'not bothered' then start populating the columns.

45. Key

What is the purpose of a key? The sole function of a key is to either lock or unlock something like a door, a box, or a window and all these things are designed to keep something inside safe and sound or to keep others out who may or may not wish to harm you. Alternatively, 'key' can be the most important element(s) of something, the key statement or 3 key parts. Being given the key to the city can mean you are trusted and respected person.

Have you ever given someone the key to your heart? We know this can go one of two ways. The other person can reciprocate this act of kindness and give you the key to their heart or if things don't quite go to plan, your heart gets broken. Remember though, life goes on regardless, yes you may be unhappy for a time, but our advice for what it's worth is to say "I'm glad they are gone. I can now find someone who truly does deserve me' and move on, go look again. You just haven't found the right person, yet.

Take a minute to consider this: "what do you believe is the key to your success?" We ask you this because it's a much more thought provoking question than "what's the secret to your success?" 'Secret' is one of those words that implies that someone is hiding something or that they know something that others don't. Most elements of success are not secret or mysterious, they are available to anyone.

There are hundreds of books, lots of audio and video clips that explain all about success. Even if you can't afford these, simply start watching successful people and ask "what is it they do that makes them successful?" Or if you get the chance to meet them, ask them yourself. Copying what they do is sure to help you. Success is a formula, and a different one for different people but none the less still a formula.

This book has been all about helping you because we know that one of the keys to being more successful is to share knowledge so that others can benefit from it. If you aim to start helping more people, more often you'll soon find this a key to improving your life.

Hmm moment:
What personal behaviours will be the key to your success in the future? Think about a few words and then make a note of them. Regularly check that you are keeping to these behaviours and you will know you're on the right route. Remember, success doesn't have to be monetary or getting a promotion it can be staying true to your ideals or morals no matter how difficult life gets.

46. Gut

Do you trust your instinct? Do you need proof, facts or evidence before you make a decision? Many people talk about gut instinct but ask them to describe what it actually is and they will struggle, saying anything from "it's just a feeling" to "its chemicals letting you know that something is right or wrong." So what is it and how can you learn to put it to best use?

People will tell you "if it looks like it's too good to be true then it probably is". Companies and people will use all kinds of advertising tactics to convince you to do or try something. They have done their research about what has an impact on people so the only way to counteract this is to do your own! Using your gut instinct effectively can be really powerful but can at times need challenging.

So how do you know if your gut instinct is right or wrong? Our best advice is to be aware of how our natural tendency is to look for evidence that backs up our initial view or perception. Say for example that you think an item in a shop is a little bit expensive, you then make comparisons with other maybe cheaper items or that maybe you could get it online cheaper. You might even make comments about the quality of the product. All this backs up your initial view because hey, nobody likes to think they are wrong!

In this scenario, maybe check out your gut instinct by asking yourself "Why might this be a good or fair price to pay?" and see what you come up with. At the end of a balanced discussion (in your head or maybe with a friend) then make your decision and see whether your gut instinct held up.

You may even find yourself doing this with people. Have you ever met someone for the first time and just didn't get a good vibe from them; something you could not quite put your finger on? You then watch their body language, listen to their words and tone of voice and observe their actions looking for something 'not good'. By doing this you might be missing out on all the evidence that they are a really nice person. It might simply be that they are very different to you and that is all your gut is telling you.

So we are not telling you to ignore your gut or instantly disregard it, we are saying listen to it but then check out what it is telling you from 2 opposite perspectives, that it might be true and that it might be false. Yes, your gut instinct can be very powerful, beyond what your logical brain is telling you but it makes sense to take it all into account.

Hmm moment:
In the next week consider what decisions you might have to make and write them down. It might be deciding which route to take on a journey, which food to buy at the supermarket or whether or not to ask a person out on a date. When each arrives, stop for a moment and ask yourself "what is my gut telling me here?"

Try at least 1-2 decisions a day and get used to tuning into your body without logically processing it in your brain. Like anything, the more you do it, the better you will get at it. Even with practice though, sometimes you will get it right, other times you won't but you will be learning from your experience and developing your skills.

47. Map

Probably the best way of helping people make sense of other people is to use the NLP (Neuro Linguistic Programming) technique or tool of 'different maps of the world'. Let us explain.

If you got out a map of your town, city, Country or of the world and asked yourself the question "is this reality or is it just a map?" We are sure you would say "it is just a map of course!" which is absolutely true. There are no fields, lakes, mountains or streets in your hand. There is just paper (or maybe a screen these days but we do like paper still). A map is simply a representation or perspective of what is there. That is pretty much the same as with us.

Our human brains each have their own 'map' of our reality, a big picture made up of all our experiences and because we have all had different experiences then our maps will be different. To one person, eating meat is a good thing on their map, to another it is a bad thing to do. The act of 'eating meat' does not change it is simply that two different maps give two different perspectives of it.

What if you had a map that was 5 years old? Would it still be an accurate representation of the landscape? Maybe things will have changed. Just because a map was once accurate does not always mean it will be. Have you ever changed your mind about something important in life?

Maybe you started seeing something using a new map that better suited you. It does not mean the old map was wrong it just means that you now have a new map. And like a current satnav system, does your map need updating? Are you still running programmes that were once useful but are now holding you back?

There is a famous phrase that says "if you do what you've always done, you'll get what you've always got". That can be true in some situations but in today's every changing world doing what you always did could be like following and old map. If you're old enough you'll remember sending memos and faxes. They were fine, they worked well. But imagine if you were still using them today.

As a child you maybe screamed when you wanted more food but you wouldn't dream of doing that now! Your map changed.

So maybe it is time to look at other areas of your life where you would like an improvement. This could be your work, relationship or health. What does your map of the 'route to fitness' look like? If it is the same one you were using 20 years ago then it is definitely out of date and there is a good chance you are still at the starting point, lost in the wilderness or have maybe gone in completely the wrong direction. And just because your best friend has a route to fitness it doesn't mean it will be right for you. As we said earlier, we create our own maps and what is right for one person is not necessarily right for anyone else.

So how else can understanding different maps help you? When having a discussion or negotiation with someone it can be extremely useful beforehand to consider 'what would their map of this situation look like?' A lot of arguments and even wars could be stopped by people acknowledging that it is actually ok to have different maps and that we need to accept others for who they are and not try to force them to accept our map as being the only correct one.

Hmm moment:

What one key person in your life would you like to better understand? Take time to really try to view life using their map. How have their childhood, work, relationships and experiences come to build their map? We are not asking you to become a psychologist but merely to experience life from a different perspective. The more you do this the more flexible and adaptable you will become which can only ever be a positive move.

48. Pay

Have you ever stopped to consider how much your life is worth? If someone offered to pay you £10 million but you would be transported 20 years into the future would you take it? Depending on who you ask you can always adjust the time and money. It is a great question to get you thinking about this. How much do you value time compared to money? Especially your own time and we all know there IS a limit to your time here on earth. But there is not a clear limit to money. The world economy in 2014 was estimated to be around $77 trillion. If you are not sure what a trillion is, well it's $1,000,000,000,000! (One trillion is a million millions!) So there is a huge amount of money out there. How much of it would you like?

Ok, you can't time-travel (and be given loads of money) but over the next 5, 10 or 20 years, you might like to consider how much you would like to earn. We have never been ones to chase the money and truly believe that you are much happier doing what you enjoy but maybe there is some level of compromise or a combination that could work. So go on, how much would you like to earn? Whatever you set as your aim you are almost sure not to earn more than that so do be generous and honestly ask yourself how much are you worth?

You might now consider whether you are likely to earn that figure in your current job, career or company.

If not and you truly believe you are worth more, then start looking around. Maybe being self-employed will pay you more than being employed but still doing pretty much the same thing. Maybe you could march up to your boss tomorrow and ask for a pay increase. Or maybe now is the time to look for a completely new career. We are not necessarily advising you to do any of these merely allowing you to consider your options. Your life really is in your hands.

When looking at your earnings you might like to also consider how you have come up with your potentials earning limit. Is it based on what your parents or friends earn? How would you feel if you earned more than all your friends put together? Actually think about that for a moment. Would you be comfortable earning that much money?

Many people say (without thinking) "oh yeah, I'd love to earn a fortune" but have no idea what it would actually be like to earn a 6 or 7 figure salary. They would probably not be comfortable handling such sums. Earning a million a year would mean taking home around £45,000 a month! That is way more than the average gross salary per annum.

Once you can buy almost anything you want you might potentially get bored and not know what to do or what to buy so if you really want to earn big, be prepared for this.

Another consideration you could make is comparing your pay to what you might pay someone else. Say you could earn £20 an hour from working and you could pay someone £10 an hour to clean your house then maybe you should work and extra hour and employ a cleaner? The same task will get done and financially you will be better off (not to mention you don't have to do boring tasks like cleaning, ironing etc.).

Many of us can't do this with a standard job unless you are regularly offered overtime but those who run their own businesses, franchises or are in network marketing may find that in the long term this truly does pay off, for what you do in the near future to improve your earnings or build your business can result in having money to invest (wisely of course) or increasing the size or scope of your business.

If you currently spend 10 hours a week doing housework (the average is 16 for working mothers) and could earn £10 an hour more than you are paying that's earning you £100 a week or £400 a month. And you are still putting in exactly the same amount of hours, just too different activities.

Act moment:
Write below how much you would really like to be earning in 5 years from now. Be realistic but be generous. Know what you want is the first step to getting it.

As you read in the chapter 'aim', without a target you are not really aiming at anything and you are highly unlikely to hit anything. And as the phrase goes "man doesn't generally find himself wandering round and ending up at the top of Everest". That's a Zig Ziglar quote. So set yourself a target now!

In 5 years from now I would like to be earning………………..

49. Act

'The most difficult thing is the decision to act, the rest is merely tenacity. The fears are paper tigers. You can do anything you decide to do. You can act to change and control your life; and the procedure, the process is its own reward' Amelia Earhart

Hopefully at this stage of the book you have found your feet and are walking a new path but in case there is still something holding you back, this chapter is for you.

Five flies are sitting on a wall, four decide to fly away. How many flies are left on the wall? One? Wrong! Five are left on the wall. Four may have decided to fly but deciding to do something and actually doing it are completely different. So what stops us taking action? Procrastination? Or maybe just forgetting? Or maybe there is just so much going on in your life that you feel like you don't have time for more?

One of the key reasons people do not take action is that the actions are in their heads and not written down. Think back to the chapters you have already read. Was there something that you were inspired to do or to change but you still haven't done it? Our guess is that you never made a plan of action. Imagine your personal challenge was to do a skydive.

Go and find your calendar or diary or open it up on your device. Now plan a date and time where you can research where you can do it and how much it will cost. Allow 30-60 minutes. Getting this in writing will make it much more likely to happen than when it's floating around in your head as an idea.

If you would like some friends to do it with you, schedule in 30 minutes when you will call or text your friends asking them to get involved. Put it in today or tomorrow. This really does not need to wait long. Now look a couple of weeks or a month ahead and enter 'review plans for skydiving'. This handy reminder will check that you are on track. Depending on what it is you are trying to achieve add as many entries as required. Break the task into manageable steps and get them written down!

So you have got your plans written but there could be something else at play. Fear. One of the main reasons people do not do what they want is fear. Fear of rejection. Fear or criticism. Fear of other people's opinions. A key questions you can ask yourself here is "what am I actually afraid of?" This will help you be really clear what the fear is. Then ask yourself "and how likely is it that this fear will come true" and "what evidence do I have that it will / will not come true?" Many of our fears are irrational or unjustified so we need to start the habit of looking for evidence.

So, some of your fears and doubts will have little evidence to back them up and you will be moving on with your plans and getting actions into your diary as previously mentioned. But sometimes you might be right. Some of your friends may judge you for taking up that odd exercise class or for trying to invent a solar powered car. Is that their issue or yours?

Who has got the issue here, the person aiming high, improving the lives of themselves and others or the person sat on their sofa judging others? We don't need to answer that! Throughout history you will find many examples of inventors, business people, musicians and politicians who were ridiculed for their ideas only to dramatically change the world. Even Harry Potter author J.K. Rowling was turned down by many publishers. Imagine if after the first few rejections she had thought "Oh well, these stories probably aren't that good then". One of the biggest franchises ever, never would have been.

Hmm moment:
Pick one of your goals or aims that you have maybe put off previously and consider what might be the biggest potential fear that could hold you back from achieving it. Take time to really consider and understand it. Now think 'what will help me get past this fear?' Try to come up with at least 2-3 things that will help you as more positive actions will help outweigh the negative ones.

50. Pen

They say 'the pen is mightier than the sword' and they are write (see what we did there?)

This well-known English saying and has been attributed to novelist and playwright Edward Bulwer-Lytton in 1839, in his historical play Cardinal Richelieu. All too often these days any writing we do, is actually typing whether text or email. That is just not the same. What we advise is to write more, maybe a journal or a book, even a thank you note or a card will do.

Depending on when you went to school you maybe have used various writing implements, a quill, a fountain pen, a biro or even a stylus. How ever you learned we would encourage you to get back to writing, not typing.

When was the last time you wrote a letter to someone? Taking the time to think about what you are going to write before you put pen to paper gives you the opportunity to really know what you want to say. Love letters may seem old fashioned now but try writing one and see the amazing impact it has on the person who receives it.

Another great thing we recommend is to keep a notebook beside your bed. This allows you at night if you are unable to sleep to capture ideas or things that are rattling around your head.

Writing things down helps to declutter and clear the mind before going to sleep. All too often we toss and turn in our beds because we all live hectic lives and have so much going on that we forget to do things. The key is to write them down. This will allow you to switch off and sleep better.

On occasions we question ourselves about all sorts of things, things like "am I good enough?" The answer we would say to you is a resounding 'Yes!' If you doing this to yourself, for whatever reason our advice is before you go to bed, get a pen and journal or notebook in hand and write down 3 things you have achieved that day. It may take a little while the first couple of times you do this but as you do it more, it will become easier and before you know it, a week then a month will pass and before long you will have 10's, then 100's of things you can be proud of.

A great technique to use when you are at work and flooded with all the jobs you need to complete is to write all the things going through your head in a list, so that you free up your mind. Two things can happen here, the first being you might actually realise you have not got as much as you first thought and secondly when you start working through the list you created you begin to cross them out when you have completed them. This second point can be incredibly satisfying. You might even do a cheeky, I'll write down an activity I have just completed and cross if off at the same time. You know what we mean.

Act moment:

Write, yes write an actual letter on paper to thank someone. Take your time mulling over what it is you want to say then put pen and we are talking a fountain pen, to paper and we are talking decent quality paper, address the envelope (that's the thing a letter goes inside before you put it through the letterbox) address it and send it snail mail. We can guarantee you the recipient will really appreciate the effort.

51. Job

There's a very good chance that you spend more of your life working than you do doing anything else whether spending time with your loved ones, taking part in sports and hobbies or even sleeping. Your job is usually what defines you. Remember the last time you met new acquaintances at a party, wedding or other social occasion, apart from the introduction and finding out their name, what was the first proper question you asked or were asked? Probably "So what do you do Jenny?" Or watch any TV game show. How do people introduce themselves? "Hi, I'm Bob and I'm an architect from Newcastle". So our job is not just what we do but also how we see ourselves. It is an important part of our identity.

So if it is so important, why leave it until chapter 51 to start thinking about work? Well yes, we agree on its importance in life but what about children, or those who are retired? How do they define themselves? And did you ever see written on someone's gravestone 'he was a really hard worker' - no, we thought not. You are far more than your job, and focusing on improving all other areas of your life will make even the most mundane or dirtiest jobs not only ok but maybe even fun or at least a challenge that you can overcome.

So, if you are going to work (after all, we do all have bills to pay) then how do you find a job or career that is right for you? And what are the options? Long gone are the days when you applied for a job after school or university and then stayed there your entire working life. Research now shows that people are not only likely to have several jobs over their lifetimes but also now, several careers too. (By the way, we didn't start out as authors as a career choice!)

Here is a simple question to get you started. Do you love doing what you do? Do you talk passionately about your role, your company and your future? Or do you moan and complain daily to anyone who will listen to you or read your Facebook posts that are obviously about your annoying boss but not explicitly so because you felt obliged to accept his or her friend request.

If you fall into the second category, then it is time to change. Use other chapters in this book to help you overcome your fears of changing roles, companies or countries.

So, you have overcome your fears, now what ARE you going to do? We think there are 2 simple questions to help you decide: Firstly, "what are you good at?" Yes, doing something that you are good at (or are willing to learn to be good at) is essential.

If you are not good at your job then you are probably not performing as well as someone else in the role could, your boss is probably not impressed and you are not really making the most of your talents and so feel held back, unfulfilled and generally miserable. No wonder you are complaining about it!

The 2nd simple question is "what do you enjoy?" Yes, enjoying your work is vital as well as complimentary to being good at it. What is it that you are passionate about? What makes you smile? What would you love to tell people at that party it is that you do?

So, it really is worth honestly answering those questions. But not only that, ask yourself about 'how' you work. This can be another important factor to finding the right work for you. Do you want to be employed or self-employed? Now it is easier than ever to set up your own online business whether selling goods or providing services and your market is global, not just local. Maybe you would rather work nights than days to fit around your family life? Have you thought of network marketing where you not only sell products or services but recruit others to do the same and then earn commission off not only what you sell but also off what your team sell. Maybe 2 part-time jobs would work better than one full-time job? Lots of choice.

In a lecture given by the late Alan Watts, he poses the question "If money was no object, what would you do for a living?" which we believe is a great way to think about it. Don't solely chase the money or you will find yourself soullessly chasing the money.

So, whatever you do, be passionate about it, because when you talk about it people with see it, feel it and get a real sense of connection when you speak. As Marc Anthony said 'If you love what you do, you'll never work another day in your life'.

Hmm moment:

Take some time to really ask yourself the two questions. "What am I good at?" and "What do I enjoy?" If you are not sure what you are good at then ask your current colleagues or manager. Sometimes others can see the strengths that are so natural to you just assume everyone has them and therefore do not recognise them in yourself.

52. Die

You might be thinking; how could they end on this one? Well let's face it, one day we will all die. There is a reason though! The following phrase can help put into context for you the time we have on earth: Look around you, in 100 years' time, everybody, yes everybody you see will be dead. This is not meant to upset you or feel negative in some way but just to jolt you into realising what a great gift / opportunity you have right now. Or if you prefer the Virgil quote: "Death twitches my ear; 'Live,' he says... 'I'm coming."

Many people talk about a 'bucket list' but many people do not have one! Start yours NOW. What do you really want to do with your life? Yes, include the big and crazy dreams but remember the small stuff too. Just seeing the smile on someone's face can mean more than seeing the Grand Canyon.

When you think about death here's a useful activity to try. Write out your own obituary or words for your headstone. We bet it doesn't say "She worked 48 hours a week in her job for 40 years and skipped lunches to fill out a spreadsheet". Does it? No. It almost always includes family and friends. The important things. We hope these are on your bucket list.

It was documented in an article that a palliative nurse in Australia asked elder people who were terminally ill what their biggest regrets were and it had nothing to do with spending more time in the office and working harder, but it was about spending time with family and loved ones. When you look back on your life do you want to have regrets? Hell, No! Before you die you want to look back on your life and think, 'what a hell of a ride' or 'I made a real difference!' Depending on your point of view.

Act moment:

Some people have a 'bucket list' over the next 7 days, write down 10 things you would like to do or achieve over the next 12 months. It can be a list of things you have never done before like skiing, horse riding, snorkeling, gone for a mountain walking or learning a new language. You need to have an aim for now. You may not do everything right away; it's about opening your mind up to the possibilities of what's out there.

End

Yes, you are at the end of the book. How lucky are we that 'end' is a three-letter word?! We hope you have taken inspiration but mostly action from this book. There may be an end to this book but we believe there is no end to personal development. It is a continual journey throughout your life. Keep learning, keep having fun, trying out new experiences and spending quality time with people that are important to you. You only get one chance at life so make every day count. It would only seem fit to end this book with 3, three-letter words so here they are... Bye for now.

Just before we go though we would like to include our thanks to a few people. Firstly, to the un-named, the countless people that have inspired, annoyed or even ignored us. Every interaction, every day gives us new learnings. Now to the people we can name!

A massive thank you to Claudine who read the book from cover to cover and help us not only spot the spelling and grammar errors but who enthused us into getting it into print.

What a great cover! Thanks Dom for designing this for us. Your technical skills are far superior to ours.

Printed in Great Britain
by Amazon